THE ARIKARA NARRATIVE OF CUSTER'S CAMPAIGN AND THE BATTLE OF THE LITTLE BIGHORN

ORIN G. LIBBY, Editor

FOREWORD BY JEROME A. GREENE
PREFACE BY DEE BROWN
INTRODUCTION BY D'ARCY McNICKLE

D1114175

UNIVERSITY OF OKLAHOMA PRESS
NORMAN

Library of Congress Cataloging-in-Publication Data

Arikara narrative of the campaign against the hostile Dakotas, June, 1876.
    The Arikara narrative of Custer's campaign and the Battle of the Little Bighorn / Orin G. Libby, editor ; foreword by Jerome A. Greene ; preface by Dee Brown ; introduction by D'Arcy McNickle.
       p.   cm.
    Originally published in 1920 under title: The Arikara narrative of the campaign against the hostile Dakotas, June, 1876.
    Includes bibliographical references and index.
    ISBN 0-8061-3072-5 (pbk. : alk. paper)
    1. Little Bighorn, Battle of the, Mont., 1876.   2. Dakota Indians—Wars, 1876.   3. Arikara Indians.   I. Libby, Orin Grant, 1864–1952. II. Title.
E83.876.A75   1998
973.8'2—dc21   98-23649
                                            CIP

Previously published under the title *The Arikara Narrative of the Campaign against the Hostile Dakotas, June, 1876.*

The paper in this book meets the guidelines for permanence and durability of the Committee on Production Guidelines for Book Longevity of the Council on Library Resources, Inc. ∞

1 2 3 4 5 6 7 8 9 10

CONTENTS

LIST OF ILLUSTRATIONS v
FOREWORD BY JEROME A. GREENE vii
PREFACE BY DEE BROWN 1
INTRODUCTION BY D'ARCY MCNICKLE 3
PREFACE 9
HISTORICAL INTRODUCTION 17
NARRATIVE OF THE ARIKARA 37
   Sitting Bear's Story 37
   Story of the First Enlistment 41
   The Narrative as continued by Soldier 46
   The Enlistment as told by Young Hawk 48
   The Second Enlistment 50
   Red Bear's Story 52
   Boy Chief's Story of His Enlistment 53
   Account of an Interview with Custer 55
   Red Star's Story of the March 57
   Story of how the Mail was brought 63
   Continuation of Red Star's Story 66
   Young Hawk's Story 69
   Red Star's Story, continued 71
   Red Star's Story of Special Scout Work 86
   Narrative of Young Hawk 93
   Supplementary Story by Soldier 115
   Continuation by Red Star, Boy Chief, and Strikes
     Two 118
   Red Star's Additional Interview 119

Supplementary Story by Red Bear 121
Later Story by Running Wolf 135
Later Story of Little Sioux 149
Later Story of Goes-Ahead 157
APPENDIX 161
  EXPEDITION TO THE BLACK HILLS 163
  GERARD'S STORY OF THE CUSTER FIGHT 171
BIOGRAPHIES 177
  SOLDIER 179
  STRIKES TWO 187
  YOUNG HAWK 193
  RED STAR 195
  RED BEAR 200
  ONE FEATHER 203
  RUNNING WOLF 204
  GOES AHEAD, CROW SCOUT 205
  JAMES COLEMAN 206
INDEX 211

ILLUSTRATIONS
(following p. 120)

LINE OF MARCH OF THE TROOPS
SITTING BEAR
LITTLE SIOUX, SOLDIER, YOUNG HAWK
GROUP OF SCOUTS
INDIAN SIGN
INDIAN SIGN LEFT BY DAKOTAS
CURLY HEAD
WAGON
SOLDIER
STRIKES TWO
LITTLE SIOUX
YOUNG HAWK
RED STAR
RED BEAR
BOY CHIEF
ONE FEATHER
RUNNING WOLF
GOES AHEAD, LITTLE BRAVE, BOB-TAILED BULL

FOREWORD

When Lieutenant Colonel George A. Custer led his Seventh Cavalry command to defeat at the Little Bighorn River in Montana in 1876, his forces included detachments of Crow and Arikara Indian scouts who guided the soldiers to their rendezvous with the Lakota (Teton Sioux) and Northern Cheyenne Indians. The Arikaras, or Rees, had been enlisted in Dakota Territory to assist the army in locating the Sioux. The Crows had been loaned to Custer days before the battle by Colonel John Gibbon, who had recruited them from their Montana agency. In the battle, the Crow and Arikara scouts were intent on capturing ponies belonging to the enemy, and some sustained casualties accompanying Major Marcus A. Reno's battalion into combat.

In the years after Little Bighorn, Indian participants in the action gave their testimony, with the Crows and Arikaras yielding accounts of the event from their perspective on the side of the U.S. soldiers. Significantly, nine Arikaras contributed translated interviews in 1912 that were published eight years later in Orin Grant Libby's "The Arikara Narrative of the Campaign against the Hostile Dakota Indians, June 1876," which formed the bulk of volume 6 of the *Collections of the State Historical Society of North Dakota*. The compilation of Arikara recollections (which also included those of one Crow scout, Goes Ahead, and a non-Indian government interpreter for the Arikaras, Frederic F. Girard) stands as a landmark in the literature of Custer's last campaign and battle.

With renewed interest in the Battle of the Little Bighorn, Indian testimony has gained acceptance and credibility. Once all but totally ignored because of their incongruity, the accounts of Lakota and Northern Cheyenne participants at the Little Bighorn have become more appreciated for their insight into the battle, especially in light of the circumstances surrounding their translation and derivation and also in view of recent archaeological evidence from the battlefield. Comparably, from the time of their availability, the statements of the Arikara participants had an immediate and long-lasting impact upon knowledge of the 1876 army expedition, including the Battle of the Little Bighorn. No serious study has failed to benefit from their manifold contributions; simply put, *The Arikara Narrative* is the most thorough and credible assembly of Indian recollections ever compiled about the campaign and battle, with many of its statements and conclusions verified by government documents.

How could any such record of Indian assertions about the Battle of the Little Bighorn be so comprehensive and so accurate? Many accounts by Lakotas and Northern Cheyennes were acquired within months or at least within several years of the events, and many commonly betrayed confusion, translation difficulties, media distortion, and fears of retribution on the part of the people who provided them (mostly warriors who had fought and killed Custer's men). Consequently, these early recollections—as such totally or partly compromised—often have been devalued by students of the Little Bighorn battle. (This by no means suggests that *all* accounts by Sioux and Northern Cheyenne veterans have been so disputed.[1]) But the Arikara interviews were different. Composed of testimony recorded decades after the events described, and with expert interpretation, they are seemingly characterized by less discord among the informants. Furthermore, the content reflects thoughts freely given by people who had been traditional enemies of the Sioux and who as scouts for the government feared little retaliation for their actions. And while the reports constitute the remembrances of but a few of the thirty-seven Arikara scouts with Custer, their stories in all likelihood would not have varied greatly with the majority on important issues of the campaign.

The Arikara Narrative is a fascinating document full of the personalities and drama of the 1876 campaign, but it is also wonderfully informal in its descriptions and sense of humor imparted by the scouts. While a valuable chronicle from the Indian viewpoint, it is—much like other treatises dealing with Custer—one not devoid of controversy. For this document contains the only known suggestion of Custer's aspiration to the presidency of the United States by one of his contemporaries (although decades after the incidents described), an Arikara scout named Red Star. Its allusion in these pages nonetheless proved sufficient for some writers to weave elaborate theses about Custer's presumed ultimate quest for political office, but in the absence of any substantive authority beyond the hearsay reference of Red Star, it remains a contention without corroboration.[2] Moreover, recent biographies of Custer that point up the man's incredible political naïveté decidedly quash this notion.[3]

Beyond this flirtation with controversy, *The Arikara Narrative* otherwise has been highly regarded as a solid source on one of the most famous events in the history of the American frontier. Since its initial publication seventy-eight years ago, *The Arikara Narrative* has sustained a following among Little Bighorn aficionados. Because of the original volume's scarcity, three private reprintings followed—two arranged by the late John M.

Carroll (J. M. Carroll Company, Mattituck, New York, 1973; and Sol Lewis, New York, 1973) and one by Rio Grande Press (Glorieta, New Mexico, 1976). This latest publication by the University of Oklahoma Press ensures that these valuable eyewitness narratives will continue to be available for historians and students of the western Indian wars. The present volume includes additional introductory material from the Sol Lewis edition. Readers desirous of additional background data on the Arikara scouts should consult John S. Gray, "Arikara Scouts with Custer," *North Dakota History: Journal of the Northern Plains* 35 (spring 1968): 442–78.

JEROME A. GREENE

Notes

1. For recent compilations of Sioux and Northern Cheyenne testimony relative to the Little Bighorn, see Jerome A. Greene, comp. and ed., *Lakota and Cheyenne: Indian Views of the Great Sioux War, 1876–1877* (Norman: University of Oklahoma Press, 1994); Richard G. Hardorff, comp. and ed., *Lakota Recollections of the Custer Fight: New Sources of Indian-Military History* (Spokane: Arthur H. Clark, 1991); and Richard G. Hardorff, comp. and ed., *Cheyenne Memories of the Custer Fight: A Source Book* (Spokane: Arthur H. Clark, 1995). A recent synthesis appears in Gregory F. Michno, *Lakota Noon: The Indian Narrative of Custer's Defeat* (Missoula, Mont.: Mountain Press Publishing, 1997).

2. For the most notable examples of this enduring myth, see Mari Sandoz, *The Battle of the Little Bighorn* (Philadelphia and New York: J. B. Lippincott, 1966); and David Humphreys Miller, *Custer's Fall: The Indian Side of the Story* (New York: Duell, Sloan, and Pearce, 1957). The most complete exposition is in Craig Repass, *Custer for President?* (Fort Collins, Colo.: Old Army Press, 1985).

3. See, in particular, Louise Barnett, *Touched by Fire: The Life, Death, and Mythic Afterlife of George Armstrong Custer* (New York: Henry Holt, 1996).

PREFACE TO
THE 1973 EDITION

The Arikara Narrative is the story of the "other Indians" at the Little Bighorn—the Arikara, Crow and Sioux scouts who served as intelligence gatherers for Custer's Seventh Cavalry. We tend to forget that Indians fought on both sides of the Revolutionary War, the War of 1812, the Civil War, and the last of our great military conflicts on American soil—the Indian Wars of the West.

Because the *Narrative* was published as one of the volumes of the North Dakota Historical Society's Collections, it received little notice as a book at its time of publication in 1920. For the same reason it has always been difficult to obtain separately from the series.

The recent upsurge of interest in the Indians' viewpoints toward the white man's conquest of the West has for the most part overlooked the role of Indian mercenaries and their attitudes. ("What made my heart jump with happiness," said one of them, "was the sight of the green paper money in my hands.") Regardless of how we may view their motives by present-day standards, their voices are important for the historical record. The Arikara scouts' first person narratives form a valuable part of the literature of the American Indian. They are also among the most important eyewitness accounts that we have of the always fascinating Custer affair on the Little Bighorn.

Thanks to O. G. Libby and other perceptive members of the North Dakota Historical Society, this important data was recorded while the participants were still living, before it became entangled in the Custer myth. The biographical notes are also useful because Indian biographies of that period are too often vague, being scanty of birth dates and blood relationships. It is unfortunate that we do not know as much about the so-called "hostiles" at the Little Bighorn as we do about the scouts.

These narratives have a special authenticity because of the care which was taken in interpretation. Too many Indian accounts have been edited and romanticized by non-Indian translators who wanted to make them seem more eloquent than they were. As Mr. Libby tells in his preface, these narratives were not only carefully translated, they were then submitted to the scouts to make certain that facts and language were correct.

From the translations we can learn what the Arikara and Crow scouts thought of various members of the famed expedition—Custer, Terry, Reynolds, Reno, Girard and others—as well as their firsthand knowledge of many disputed points concerning the now legendary battle. Although the accounts are all by Arikaras, they tell us a great deal about the Crows who came with Gibbon from the west and were then attached to Custer's command, and of the Sioux mercenaries who rode with the expedition from Fort Abraham Lincoln.

DEE BROWN
Urbana, Illinois

INTRODUCTION TO
THE 1973 EDITION

Rarely have Indians had the opportunity to tell in their own words the story of their participation in a significant historical event, and this reprint of *The Arikara Narrative of the Campaign Against the Hostile Dakotas, June, 1876,* is important on that account, apart from the events described.

The narrative, which tells of the Custer campaign and its disastrous culmination at the battle of the Little Bighorn, consists of the personal accounts of nine survivors of the group of forty Arikara scouts attached to the United States 7th Cavalry before and during that campaign. The material was gathered by the North Dakota Historical Society in 1912, some thirty-six years after the events described, the incidents of which are recalled with remarkable clarity and minuteness of detail. Each informant told his story in his own language, which was translated and written out in English, and afterward read back to the narrator for confirmation. Since the Arikara interpreter, Peter Beauchamp, had attended Hampton Institute, precursor to the Carlisle Indian School, the rendering into English has the flavor of Indian talk, even something of the humor of Indian story-telling.

The narrators spent four summer days together at the home of one of their number on the Fort Berthold Reservation, North Dakota, each one telling the story of his personal experience in the engagement. At one point during these recitations, one of the scouts went out of the house and was heard singing a wailing song. He was unhappily recalling that the horse he rode on that fateful day was so heavy-footed and slow that he had been left behind when his fellows charged into battle. The recorder commented: "No one inside paid the slightest attention although we could hardly hear what the interpreter was saying."

For those who are distressed by the seeming lack of a moral code that allowed the Indians of one tribe to sell their services to the white man's army in action against another tribe, the incidents of the *Arikara Narrative* offer some countering insights.

The campaign against the Sioux-Cheyenne coalition was, for the Arikara tribesmen, but one incident in the long campaign against marauding Plains Indians. The Arikara with their linguistic kinsmen, the Pawnee, had been village dwelling, farming Indians for several centuries before the horse came to the central Plains at the beginning of the 18th century. Thereafter, the village dwellers and their gardens were prime targets for mounted hunters in search of food. The Arikara retreated up the Missouri River late in the century to evade the constant raids launched upon them, but they found no asylum in the north. When Custer requested scouts to assist in defeating the Sioux, he found willing volunteers among the Arikara men, who saw a chance to settle old scores. The Sioux, apparently, reacted in like spirit. The Arikara scouts killed on the Little Bighorn were badly battered, as were the white soldiers who died that day. They were even stripped of their serviceable army clothing.

Except for their momentary involvement with the United States army in that summer of 1876, the Arikara and their neighbors on the Missouri were living out their lives as best they could, holding to those values, such as bravery in battle, which made life worthwhile, and practicing the skills essential to their survival. Under other circumstances they might have fought against the army, as once they had attacked white men coming up the river.

One other dimension must be considered in judging the moral behavior of those tribesmen who fought on the side of white men against other tribes. While it is common practice to use the term "Indian" in referring to the aboriginal population of the New World, the people in reference had no reason to think of themselves as being one people, and therefore they had no need of a common name. Each group, by whatever name it called itself, had a separate history, a defined territory, and a language which might by chance be shared with others, near or far. Even the sharing of a language created no necessary affinity. The several Apache bands could raid each other as readily as they raided a Mexican village, and experience no sense of disloyalty. The hunting tribes of the plains, the deserts, and the far north perforce operated in small groups, often consisting of no more than an extended family, and primary loyalty was to the cohabiting group, with extensions to a kinship lineage and, more remotely, to a geographically defined band of interrelated kinsmen. Beyond that was a world of strangers, potentially hostile.

Tribes or bands often overcame their distrust of outsiders and formed alliances, usually temporary, but sometimes lasting through generations. Such was the alliance of the Arikara with the Mandan and the Hidatsa Indians on the Missouri River—all having a tradition of settled village life, and all greatly reduced in population as a result of epidemics and the pillaging of nomadic Plains tribes. The need for mutual defense against common enemies was great enough in this instance to overcome language barriers, since the Mandan and Hidatsa spoke different Siouan dialects and the Arikara were Caddoan speakers.

Out of such native experience, and out of pressing need, the idea of entering into a temporary alliance with the United States army involved no moral question. The Arikara scouts enlisted to carry out a task well within their training and custom—which was to capture enemy horses. The fact that they failed in their mission, were caught within enemy fire and some were killed, was part of the risk which they understood, and invited.

The personality of Custer, the man, emerges in sympathetic detail in these accounts. Thus, the scout, Red Star, comments: "Here Gerard [an interpreter, speaking for Custer] told us he wanted us to sing our death song. The Dakota trail had been seen and the fight would soon be on. Custer had a heart like an Indian; if we ever left out one thing in our ceremonies he always suggested it to us. We got on our horses and rode around, singing the songs. Then we fell in behind Custer and rode on."

When a scout disputed a Custer decision, evidently without hesitation, the Colonel answered, at first "angrily," then thought better of his decision after further discussion, and agreed. "Yes," he said, "it shall be done as you say."

The Historical Introduction provides a concise but informative review of the events leading up to the Little Bighorn and the disaster that followed. It is a dispassionate account, reflecting neither the praise nor blame for what happened that June day. The Indian accounts are equally devoid of subjective judgments but, carefully studied in the context of the total action, they are seen as a critical commentary on the nature of the Custer debacle. It should be mentioned further that the Indian stories are alive with details of heroic acts and human miscalculation. Red Bear's hilarious account of how he fared in battle, repeatedly falling off his horse at crucial moments and having his riding gear snagged in the underbrush, to his embarrassment, is the perfect portrait of the non-hero in action.

If Indians had been writing their own histories of their encounters with the white man, our knowledge of how the West was won would be better balanced and more believable. The reprinting of this document contributes to that better understanding.

D'ARCY McNICKLE
Center for the History of the American Indian
The Newberry Library, Chicago

PREFACE

The purpose in publishing this material on the Indian campaign of 1876 is twofold. Merely as a matter of justice to the Arikara Indian scouts their version of the campaign in which they played an important part should have long ago been given to the public. Nearly every other conceivable angle of this memorable campaign has received attention and study. But during the past generation the Arikara scouts, true to their oath of fealty to the government as they understood it, have remained silent as to their own part in those eventful days. The present narrative is designed to make public the real story of the Arikara Indian scouts who served with Terry and under the immediate command of Custer.

In August, 1912, the nine survivors of some forty of these scouts met at the home of Bear's Belly on the Fort Berthold Reservation, at Armstrong, and there they related to Judge A. McG. Beede and to the secretary of the State Historical Society the various portions of the narrative that follow. Each of the scouts gave that special portion of the whole with which he was most familiar. The narrators were very scrupulous to confine themselves to just that portion of the common experience to which they were eye witnesses. While it was not always possible to maintain this rule in every part of the narrative, yet for the most part what is set down in this account is the testimony of those who were actual participants. The narratives were carefully taken down as interpreted by Peter Beauchamp, a graduate of Hampton Institute, Virginia. After the whole story was put in form it was submitted to the Indians to be read and corrected through their interpreters by all those who had taken part. Thus there has been assembled a complete account of these important events given from the standpoint of an Indian scout. While it is true that these scouts knew nothing of the general plan of the campaign nor of the larger features of the movements in which they took part, nevertheless they have supplied an astonishing number of clear cut facts and observations that have all the definiteness and accuracy of an instantaneous photograph.

In the second place the narratives of individual scouts and their accompanying biographies give us a vivid insight into the life of a few individuals and families under actual conditions as they existed on our reservations. The true Indian is extremely reticent concerning matters of ritual, family tradition, and tribal observance. Not as much of such details was obtained as was asked for, still the narrative affords, in many instances, a flashlight picture of Indian life.

Among the valuable records collected while the narrative was being secured is a set of phonographic records made of the Arikara songs used during the battles or composed in honor of Custer and the scouts who were killed by the Dakotas. We were privileged to hear, also, a large number of other rare and remarkable ceremonial chants and songs, but the scouts did not allow them to be recorded.

At the close the occasion was celebrated by the organization of a society known as the U. S. Volunteer Indian Scouts, in imitation of the G. A. R. Two local posts are already in existence, to which belong most of the veteran scouts of the Fort Berthold Reservation, including those who had enlisted subsequent to the campaign of 1876.

An impartial examination of the evidence offered in the narrative of these scouts will completely clear them from the old charge of cowardice which has so long been voiced against them. These scouts were charged with being responsible for the defeat of Reno's men in their first encounter with the Dakotas at the upper village on the Little Big Horn. The evidence points clearly to the fact that the thin line of Arikara scouts extending from where the soldiers stood out to the left was overwhelmed and rolled up by a mass of Dakota horsemen who rode out from behind some low hills farther to the left. Of these scouts, Bob-tailed Bull was the first to fall and he stood until the attack came, far out to the left, a solitary horseman facing scores of circling warriors. The second leader of the scouts, Bloody Knife, also took a prominent part in the preliminary skirmishing and he was finally killed by a shot from a Dakota marksman on the high ground to the rear of Reno's position. All of the scouts, when asked their opinion regarding the retreat of the troops from the strong position behind a cut bank on the edge of the timber, were emphatic in maintaining that Reno could have held this well protected position indefinitely. According to Judge A. McG. Beede, who is well acquainted with the Dakotas, these Indians, also, held the same view.

The vigorous efforts made by the scouts to drive off the pony herd of the Dakotas is justified by their understanding of Custer's orders to that effect which they have given in detail. That they paid more attention to this portion of their orders was simply the result of the fact that they understood that the pony herd was vitally important in the fighting power of the Dakotas. That they failed in their skillful and gallant attempt to carry out the orders of their chief lay not in their lack of courage but from the fact that Reno's soldiers failed to hold their own strong line of defense on the other side of the river. This released swarms of Dakota horsemen who crossed the river and swept down upon the handful of scouts who had already started to drive off the pony herd and sent them scurrying for safety to the high ground overlooking the river.

After Benteen had joined his command with Reno's
there does not seem to have been anyone able or
willing to give the scouts any order as to their next
move. Left to themselves they fell back upon their
last order from Custer, that in case of defeat they
were to retreat to the base camp. On this retreat
they attempted once more to drive off a herd of Dakota ponies that had previously been assembled by
various scouts during the earlier part of the day.
The Crow scouts tell a somewhat similar story.
They speak of their dismissal by Custer after his
command was ready to move to the attack. He left
them free to stay or go as they saw fit.

This brings out a fact which Custer understood
very well and upon which he planned his strategy.
He never used his scouts for line fighting. They
were trained, as he well knew, for skirmishing, for
trailing, for capturing the pony herds of the enemy.
In planning this last of his battles he depended
upon the scouts to show him the enemy and, if possible, to cripple the fighting power of the force op-
posed to him by capturing or stampeding their
horses. From every detail of this long narrative,
Custer's scouts seem to have performed their part
with skill and courage. They even gave such fine
examples of personal prowess as those related of
Bob-tailed Bull, Bloody Knife, and Young Hawk.
That Custer's plan of battle broke down can not in
all fairness be ascribed to any failure on the part
of his devoted scouts who carried out his orders in

a manner which, had he lived, would have elicited from him the warmest commendation. We may well leave to military experts the task of pointing out the defects in the strategy and in the conduct of the battle of the Little Big Horn. All that this present narrative expects to accomplish is to supply the facts upon which we may base a judgment regarding the behavior of Custer's Arikara scouts. That they faced a difficult task and attempted to carry out his orders against heavy odds seems fairly well attested by the evidence. From a complete misunderstanding of the duty Custer assigned to these scouts, military men have pretty generally minimized their services and laid them under the heavy charge of cowardice in the face of the enemy. Custer understood them perfectly and did not expect them to do more than what they did. That they did not feel themselves guilty of any failure to carry out orders is evident from the straightforward character of their various narratives. The same impression was given in listening to their own words and watching their facial expression as they reviewed, bit by bit, throughout the long four days' session, the part they had played in the events leading up to the loss of their great benefactor and friend.

Quite different is the impression made as to the parts played by Black Fox, the Arikara scout, and Curly, the Crow scout. The false and absurd claims made by Curly that he was the sole survivor of the

Custer fight are absolutely repudiated by his fellow scouts and even the Arikara scouts are aware of his untrustworthiness. By the testimony of the only Arikara scout to leave the field before the fight began, Curly, his companion, did what Custer had told the other Crow scouts to do. By what accident or design he has been made to appear, perhaps innocently at first, as the sole survivor of Custer's command, has not yet been made to appear. That the other Crow scouts look upon him with contempt as an imposter is beyond question.

The present volume is offered as a piece of evidence worthy of being included in the source material for the future study of this period of our history. It may serve, also, as a demonstration of the value and credibility of such first-hand testimony in any research that may be conducted in this field.

HISTORICAL INTRODUCTION

In the year 1867 Congress provided for a commission composed of four civilians and three army officers who were to treat with all the Indian tribes of the Great Plains and arrange a treaty which would grant to them definite lands. This, it was thought, would cause them to settle down and cease their war on the white man. Parts of two years were spent in visiting the scattered bands and finally, in April, 1868, an agreement was concluded which defined clearly the boundaries of the territory set apart for the Dakotas.[1] This area was not large when compared with the fields over which the Dakotas had been accustomed to roam at will, but it included the Black Hills and adjacent lands which they had cherished for a long time as a hunt-

---

[1] The United States set apart reservation for their occupancy as follows: ''Commencing on the east bank of the Missouri river where the 46th parallel of north latitude crosses it; thence along low-water mark down said east bank to a point opposite where the north line of the state of Nebraska strikes said river; thence west across said river and along said northern line of Nebraska to the 104th meridian; thence north along said meridian to the 46th parallel of north latitude; thence east along said parallel to the place of beginning. Said Indians relinquish all right to occupy territory outside the above defined reservation, but reserve the right to hunt on any lands north of North Platte and on the Republican Fork of Smoky Hill River so long as buffalo may range there in numbers sufficient to justify the chase.''—U. S. Bureau of Am. Ethnology. *Annual Report, 1896-1897*, XVIII, p. 848.

ing ground and asylum. Consequently when gold
was discovered in these hills and when the expedition commanded by Colonel Geo. A. Custer was
sent "to reconnoiter the route from Fort Abraham
Lincoln to Bear Butte," a well known point north
of the Black Hills, and "to explore the country
south, southeast, and southwest of that point," the
Indians were much disturbed.

This expedition had been organized at Fort Lincoln in June, and since the trails from the camp of
the hostile Dakotas on the Yellowstone to the Indian reservation agencies near the Missouri led by
a southeasterly course through the hills, it was considered desirable to obtain positive and accurate information regarding them and "to connect them as
well by reconnaisance with the posts of Lincoln and
Laramie."[2] Colonel Custer was directed to proceed by the route which he would find most desirable to Bear Butte or some other point on or near
the Belle Fourche, and thence push explorations in
such directions as in his judgment would enable
him to obtain the most information in regard to the
character of the country and the possible routes of
communication through it. He was directed to return to Fort Lincoln within sixty days from the
time of his departure from it, but he was author-

[2] The expedition consisted of six companies of the Seventh Cavalry
stationed at Fort Lincoln; four companies of the same regiment then
stationed at Fort Rice; Company I, Twentieth Infantry; and Company
G, Seventeenth Infantry; together with sixty-one Indian scouts from
Fort Lincoln and Fort Rice selected by the commander of the expedition.

ized to return from any point of his contemplated
march, even before the Belle Fourche would be
reached, if any unforeseen obstacle made it necessary or advisable.

The expedition started from Fort Lincoln on
July 2, 1874, taking a southwesterly course. It was
able to explore the cave about which the Indian
scouts had told so many wonderful stories. This
cave was found in the eastern side of a ridge several miles long, covered with pine. It was a hole
washed out of the sandstone two or three hundred
feet in depth horizontally, with an entrance fifteen
by twenty feet, and it proved to possess no special
interest other than that imparted to it by the super-
stitions of the Indians. When the valley of the
Belle Fourche was reached, July 19th, the command
remained in camp. The distance marched from
Fort Lincoln was 292 miles, an average of 18¼
miles per day. The Indians were reluctant about
entering the hills, protesting that the wagons could
not be taken further. They had supposed the expedition would not seriously attempt an entrance,
but would only skirt the hills. However, on July
20th, the first day's journey was made into the
hills. The course led southward up the valley of
the Red Water, a branch of the Belle Fourche; and
a well-marked pony and lodge trail led up the valley
southeasterly to the Red Cloud and Spotted Tail
Agencies. An old badly cut lodge trail was discovered which, according to the scouts, was originally

an old voyageur pack-trail; and it was one of the routes between the hostile camp on the Tongue River and the agencies. On the afternoon of the 26th, a Dakota village of seven lodges was found. Custer wanted these Indians to guide his party through the hills but at nightfall they abandoned their camp and made their escape. Their chief, One Stab, was in Custer's camp when their flight was discovered and he was detained as a guide and hostage. His wife was the daughter of Red Cloud.

On the 3d of August, Charles Reynolds, a white scout, was sent to Fort Laramie with dispatches. He made the seventy-five-mile trip with only a compass to guide him through a country infested with Indians. He suffered great hardship due to lack of water. Fort Laramie, a very old frontier post on the left bank of the Laramie River, about two miles from its junction with the North Platte, and just at the foot of the northeastern slope of the Laramie Range of the Rockies, was originally a station of the Hudson's Bay Company and later a station and trading post of the American Fur Company. It was first occupied by the United States as a military post in 1849.

On August 6th, camp was broken for the return trip. Colonel Custer decided to partly retrace his route, instead of going eastward upon the prairie, as he desired to discover if a northward route through the hills, emerging somewhere near Bear Butte, was practicable. So the old trail was followed with but slight divergence. During the return four Cheyenne Indians were encountered on their way to the agencies from the hostile camp on the Tongue River. They asserted that Sitting Bull with 5,000 warriors was preparing to intercept the expedition at Short Pine Hills, but nothing was seen of them. On August 20th the march led north and west over a rolling prairie which the Indians had burned over to embarrass the expedition and which necessitated a descent into the Little Missouri Valley, where the Bad Lands begin, for wood, water, and grass. The command worked gradually out of the burnt district on the 27th and crossed the Heart River at noon, August 30th. The wagon train had traveled 883 miles; the men had marched nearly 1,000 miles and the total number of miles surveyed was 1,205. The evidence gathered on the trip with regard to a large amount of precious metal in the Black Hills was on the whole discouraging. But otherwise, the expedition was in every way successful and it made a large addition to the existing knowledge of the country, which was likely to be of value in case of hostilities with the Dakotas.

Other expeditions followed, and soon there began a rush of white men into this territory.[3] It was at

---

[3] The question of gold in the Black Hills was not considered settled by the expedition of 1874; therefore in 1875 another expedition was sent out by the Interior Department, headed by Walter P. Jenny, a mining engineer, escorted by an ample force of troops under Colonel R. I. Dodge.— *Report of the Commissioner of Indian Affairs, 1875*, Wash., 1875, p. 8.

this point that the Indians were aroused and made a desperate attempt to defend their lands and their rights in the treaty.

From the time of the treaty of 1868 there had remained outside of the reservation a number of Dakotas, known as hostiles. To these were constantly being added outlaws who left the reservations, until the number which could be called hostile was probably about three thousand. Most of these were under the leadership of Sitting Bull. In November, 1875, the commissioner of Indian affairs reported "it will probably be necessary to compel the northern non-treaty Sioux, and such outlaws from the several agencies as have attached themselves to these same hostiles, to cease marauding and settle down, as the other Sioux have done."[4] The Indian inspector, E. C. Watkins, after investigation advised that troops be sent against these hostile Indians "that winter; the sooner the better," and that the force consist of a thousand men. Accordingly General Sheridan, in whose division these Indians were, instructed General Crook to prepare for the expedition.[5] But in December the secretary of the

[4] *Report of Secretary of War, 1876*, Wash., 1876, I, p. 28.

[5] In 1876, the territory of the United States was divided into three military divisions, namely, the Missouri, the Atlantic, and the Pacific. The division of the Missouri embraced the states and territories bordering on the Mississippi and Missouri Rivers, extending westward so as to include substantially the entire Rocky Mountain chain, and was commanded by Lieut. Gen. P. H. Sheridan, with his headquarters in Chicago and was composed of five different departments. The first was that of Dakota, commanded by Brig. Gen. A. H. Terry, with his headquarters

interior stated that it was his purpose to send out runners to notify these Indians that they must come in to their reservations by or before the 31st of January, 1876, or a military force would be sent against them. On the first day of February, when the time given the hostiles had expired, the secretary of the interior formally turned them over to the military authorities for such action as they might deem proper under the circumstances, and General Sheridan then instructed General Crook to proceed to reduce these Indians to subjection. This officer, and Colonel J. J. Reynolds with an expedition numbering 883 men, went into the Rosebud and Powder Horn countries. Here the group was divided into two parts. Colonel Reynolds followed the trail of two Indians and struck the camp of Crazy Horse, one of the hostile bands. The Indians fled, the soldiers destroyed the camp, while being shot at from rocks, bushes, and gullies, and then they returned to the place where they were to meet General Crook. Together they went back to Fort Fetterman, reaching that place March 26th.

The results of this expedition were neither conclusive nor satisfactory, since General Crook was

at St. Paul; the second that of the Platte, commanded by Brig. Gen. George Crook, with headquarters at Omaha; the third that of the Missouri, commanded by Brig. Gen. John Pope, with headquarters at Fort Leavenworth; the fourth that of Texas, commanded by Brig. Gen. E. O. C. Ord, with headquarters at San Antonio; the fifth that of the Gulf, commanded by Brig. Gen. C. C. Augur, with headquarters at New Orleans. *Report of Secretary of War, 1876*, Wash., 1876, I, p. 25.

driven back by the Indians, and General Sheridan now determined to carry out a systematic campaign. Accordingly he ordered three distinct divisions, General Crook (who had recovered from his winter's defeat) from the Platte, General Terry from Dakota, and Colonel Gibbon from Montana, to march simultaneously toward a common center, that common center to be near the Big Horn River, a tributary of the Yellowstone.

The military authorities assumed that any one of these three divisions could defeat the enemy, the only difficulty being to catch him, for it was believed that no one of the commanders would encounter more than five or eight hundred hostile warriors. But the failure of Crook's expedition in March, and the delay of Custer's command at Fort Lincoln, had caused hundreds of Indians to slip away from the Red Cloud and Spotted Tail reservations in Nebraska, and from their reservations on the Missouri, so that Sitting Bull's camp as Custer found it contained approximately twenty-five hundred to three thousand warriors from all the different tribes of the Dakota nation. They were supplied with fine rifles and had large quantities of ammunition. Many of these were outlaws, but the worst feature of the matter was that the agents at the reservations had concealed the fact that numerous bands had left their reservations.

On the 29th of May, the division under General Crook, consisting of two battalions of the Second

and Third Cavalry commanded by Lieutenant
Colonel W. B. Royall and a battalion of five companies of the Fourth and Ninth Infantry under
Major Alex. Chambers, marched northward from
Fort Fetterman on the Platte, to Goose Creek, head
of Tongue River, a tributary of the Yellowstone.
Here he established his supply camp June 8th.
Moving from this camp on the 16th, toward the
headwaters of the Rosebud, another tributary of
the Yellowstone, General Crook encountered, June
17th, a large number of Indians commanded by
Red Cloud, forty miles north of Goose Creek, and
was so badly crippled that he retreated the next day
to his supply camp to await reënforcements and
supplies, practically eliminated from the campaign.[6]

Colonel John Gibbon, with his division consisting of four companies of the Second Cavalry and
six companies of the Seventh Infantry (total 450
men), marched from Fort Ellis in Montana eastward along the north bank of the Yellowstone
River to the mouth of the Rosebud, to meet General Alfred H. Terry. The infantry started March
30th, and the cavalry April 1st. General Terry,
with the Seventh Cavalry under its lieutenant-
colonel, Geo. A. Custer, was stationed at Fort Abraham Lincoln, near Bismarck. This command con-

---

[6] Sheridan in his report gives the date when Crook moved from
Goose River as June 13th. The correct date was June 16th as stated
in the reports of both Sherman and Crook. *Report of Secretary of War,
1876*, Wash., 1876, I, pp. 30, 442, 504.

sisted of twelve companies of the Seventh Cavalry, twenty-eight officers, and about seven hundred men; two companies of the Seventeenth U. S. Infantry, and one company of the Sixth U. S. Infantry, eight officers and one hundred five men; one platoon of three gatling guns; two officers and thirty-two men of the Twentieth U. S. Infantry, and forty Arikara Indian scouts.

On the morning of May 17th this command started on its ill-fated expedition. The first halt was made near the Little Missouri where Custer, with four troops, went on a reconnoitering trip up the valley. On June 1st and 2d they were delayed by a snow storm, but they reached the mouth of the Powder River June 10th. From here Major Reno, with a part of Custer's army, was sent to reconnoiter, and Custer went on to the mouth of the Tongue River to which place Reno returned, June 19th, bringing news of a "large Indian trail" leading up the Rosebud. There were many indications that the Indians' stronghold was upon the Little Big Horn about fifteen miles above its junction with the Big Horn. Custer reached the mouth of the Rosebud on June 21st. Here he was met by General Terry who had gone up the Yellowstone on the supply steamer. General Gibbon also joined them here, having left his command near the mouth of the Big Horn. A conference was held on board the steamer "Far West" at which it was decided that Custer with the Seventh Cavalry should follow the Indian trail discovered by Reno, while the others were to continue to the mouth of the Big Horn where Custer was to report later. The written instructions given to Custer were as follows:

CAMP AT THE MOUTH OF THE ROSEBUD RIVER,
Montana Territory.

June 22, 1876.

LIEUTENANT-COLONEL CUSTER, 7th Cavalry.

Colonel: The Brigadier-General Commanding directs that, as soon as your regiment can be made ready for the march, you will proceed up the Rosebud in pursuit of the Indians whose trail was discovered by Major Reno a few days since. It is, of course, impossible to give you any definite instructions in regard to this movement, and were it not impossible to do so the Department Commander places too much confidence in your zeal, energy, and ability to wish to impose upon you precise orders which might hamper your action when nearly in contact with the enemy. He will, however, indicate to you his own views of what your action should be, and he desires that you should conform to them unless you shall see sufficient reason for departing from them. He thinks that you should proceed up the Rosebud until you ascertain definitely the direction in which the trail above spoken of leads. Should it be found (as it appears almost certain that it will be found) to turn toward the Little Big Horn, he thinks that you should still proceed southward perhaps as far as the headwaters of the Tongue, and then turn towards the Little Horn, feeling constantly, however, to your left, so as to preclude the possibility of the escape of the Indians to the south or southeast by passing around your left flank. The column of Colonel Gibbon is now in motion for the mouth of the Big Horn. As soon as it reaches that point it will cross the Yellowstone and move up at least as far as the forks of the Big and Little Horns. Of course its future movements must be controlled by circumstances as they arise, but it is hoped that the Indians, if upon the Little Horn, may be so nearly inclosed by the two columns that their escape will be impossible.

The Department Command desires that on your way up the Rosebud you should thoroughly examine the upper part of Tulloch's Creek, and that you should endeavor to sent a scout through to Colonel Gibbon's column, with information of the result of your examination. The lower part of this creek will be examined by a detachment from Colonel Gibbon's command. The supply steamer will be pushed up the Big Horn as far as the forks, if the river is found to be navigable for that distance, and the Department Commander, who will accompany the column of Colonel Gibbon, desires you to report to him there not later than the expiration of the time for which your troops are rationed, unless in the meantime you receive further orders.

Very respectfully, your obedient servant,

E. W. SMITH, Captain 18th Infantry,

Acting Assistant Adjutant-General.

Having received these instructions, the Seventh Cavalry and its accompanying party of Arikara and Crow scouts marched out of camp at noon on June 22d. In consultation with its officers that evening, Custer took unusual precautions to provide for secrecy. During the first day's march three large Indian camping places were passed. June 24th was a tedious, dusty day, and the troops made long halts to keep in touch with the scouts, who were carefully examining the country, especially on the right towards Tulloch's Creek as Terry had ordered. Many more forsaken camping places were passed this day and instead of realizing, as he should have done, that these were the camps of an unusually large number of Indians, Custer, probably influenced by the reports of military authorities that there were not more than five or eight hundred warriors in this hostile band, mistook these numerous camps for a succession of camps of the same or a few villages.

In the largest of these forsaken camps, a large sun dance lodge was standing. It contained a white man's scalp. At sundown, after marching about twenty-eight miles, a camp was made under cover of a bluff. General Custer seemed strangely depressed, and that evening, departing from his usual custom, he consulted with his officers. He informed them that the trail led over the divide between the Rosebud and the Little Big Horn Rivers, and that the march would be continued at once for he was anxious to get to the divide before daylight. After marching about ten miles, he halted the command a little after 2 A.M., June 25th, and waited news from the Arikara scouts, who, with the chief scout, Lieutenant Varnum, were reconnoitering. He was of course anxious that these scouts should definitely locate the enemy in their camp, and that the enemy should not be aware of his approach. After a much needed rest of five and one-half hours they moved on cautiously for a distance of ten miles, and halted again in a ravine concealed from view. This ravine was about a mile from the Little Chetish or Wolf Mountains, a high, broken, and rough country of precipitous hills and deep narrow gulches which form the divide between the Little Big Horn and the Rosebud. Looking from the high hills at this point the Indian scouts discovered the Dakota village in the Little Big Horn Valley, which they concluded was twelve or fifteen miles away. But with this news they also reported that the Indians had evidently discovered the approach of the white men, for the group nearest Custer's command was moving away. Later they learned that this was but a smaller camp joining the larger one down the valley.

However, Custer, fearing that the Indians were moving away, and thinking that there were not more than eight hundred Indian warriors in the country, decided to attack at once as delay would allow the village to scatter and escape. After an inspection of the troops, the column started and crossed the divide a little before noon. Shortly afterwards the command was divided into three parts,[7] one under Reno, one under Custer, and a third under Benteen. The pack-train was under the escort of McDougall with Troop B.

Reno's battalion marched down a valley that developed into a small tributary of the Little Big Horn now called Benteen's Creek. Custer's column and the pack-train followed closely, but Benteen was ordered to the left and front, to a line of high hills three or four miles distant, where the country was exceedingly rough and hard on his horses. The first two battalions did not meet any Indians until they arrived at a burning tepee, probably fired by the scouts, and here they saw a few. They did not act surprised, nor did they make any attempt to delay the troops. They simply kept far enough ahead to invite pursuit.

The Indian village was strung along the west bank of the Little Big Horn for a distance of three or four miles. When the troops were close to the river, Custer ordered Reno to move forward at as rapid a gait as he thought prudent, and "charge the village." Reno moved off at a trot toward the river, delayed ten or fifteen minutes watering the horses, then crossed the stream and reformed his column on the left bank with the Arikara scouts on

[7] Godfrey, *Custer's Last Battle*, N. Y., 1892, 368.

his left. Advancing about a mile further, he met with little resistance. Then the Indians opened a brisk fire and made a dash toward the left where the scouts were. Here Reno, instead of obeying his commands and charging the village as he had been ordered to do, to throw the Indians into confusion and destroy a part of their village, halted, dismounted his troops, and fought on foot until he was forced back into the timber. This position was a strong one and he remained there till nearly surrounded, when he gave the order to mount and get to the bluffs. This order was not generally understood and a confused retreat followed. He was forced to the left by the attack and did not get to the ford by which he had entered the valley. He found a fordable place, but by this time the command had lost all semblance of organization and a number of men were killed before they reached the bluffs.

Meanwhile, Benteen had gone to the left over a succession of high hills and deep valleys. The farther he advanced, the more difficult the way became. During this march his men could get occasional glimpses of the Custer battalion, distinguished by the troop mounted on gray horses. Before he had gone too far over this rugged country, Benteen decided to follow the trail of the rest of the command and turning back, reached it just before the pack-train. Shortly afterwards he received a message from Custer telling him to hurry on to join his command. Benteen's march brought him to the bluffs where he met Reno's retreating troops and his battalion was ordered to dismount and deploy as skirmishers along the valley.[8] The Indians soon withdrew from this attack, presumably in order to give their whole attention to Custer, who was by this time separated from the other troops by a distance of two and one-half or three miles.

Custer, on leaving Reno, had gone to the right of the river and the ridge down a ravine that led to the river. Some of Reno's men had seen a party of Custer's command, including Custer himself, on the bluffs about the time the Indians began to develop their attack on Reno's front. This party was heard to cheer, and the men were seen to wave their hats as if to give encouragement, and they then disappeared behind the hills. It is probable that from this ridge, Custer saw plainly the Indian village, and realized that the chances were desperate. Reno was already in the fight, and Custer had no reason to think that he would not push his attack vigorously; accordingly it was about this time that the messenger was sent to Benteen with Custer's last order, "Benteen, come on. Big village. Be quick. Bring packs. Cook, Adjutant. P.S. Bring packs."

For a long time after Benteen joined Reno, firing was heard down the river in the vicinity of Custer's command. Benteen's three companies had doubled

---

[8] Godfrey, *Custer's Last Battle*, p. 372.

Reno's force and with the company of the pack-train, which arrived a little later, there were seven companies under Reno, while Custer had only five. Custer's need of supplies and men was shown by his urgent message to Benteen, and if these seven companies with their ammunition had hastened to his aid, their united force might have enabled Custer to save his command. The attack on Custer's command lasted but a short time, and no survivor was left to tell the story of the fight. An examination of the field, however, gave evidence of the stubborn resistance offered by the troops.

After the annihilation of Custer's command the Indians turned their attention to Reno who was moving out in Custer's direction. He was driven back to the ridge and the Indians continued to fire upon his command till dark, when they stopped to celebrate their victory by a scalp dance in the valley below. Some of the scouts were sent out after dark to look for signs of Custer's command but they returned after a short absence to report that the country was full of the enemy. The next morning the Indians renewed the attack, the soldiers dug shallow rifle pits and piled up boxes of hard tack across the most exposed portion of their position. They suffered much from thirst as the Indians carefully guarded the river to prevent any water from being obtained. Later in the afternoon the firing grew slack and about 3 o'clock it ceased altogether. It is thought that their runners must have brought to the Indians news of the approaching column, for Terry with Gibbon's command arrived about 11 o'clock on Tuesday morning. Reno and his men had seen the Indians moving away at dusk, but did not then know the cause. The timely arrival of Terry, without doubt, saved Reno and his command from a fate like that of Custer's.

Thus the expedition, so carefully planned, and so confident of victory, had completely failed. The Indians had succeeded in hiding their strength from the scouts and were able to go into battle with at least three times as many warriors as Custer had expected to find. The principal war chief engaged in the battle was Gall, of the Hunkpapas. Other important leaders were Crow King and Black Moon of the same band; Low Dog, Crazy Horse, and Big Road of the Oglalas; Lame Deer, leading the Minniconjous, and Hump of the same band; White Bull and Little Horse of the Cheyennes, and Spotted Eagle of the Sans-Arcs. Gall, Crow King, and Crazy Horse played the leading part, while Sitting Bull, though important in the councils, took no part in the battle.[9]

---

[9] It is impossible to ascertain with any certainty the whereabouts of Sitting Bull during the battle of the Little Big Horn. Various writers differ in their accounts and the Indians when questioned on the subject remain silent.

NARRATIVE OF THE ARIKARA

OF THEIR PART IN THE CAMPAIGN OF LIEUT.-COL. GEORGE A. CUSTER, JUNE, 1876

Sitting Bear's Story of his father, Son-of-the-Star, in the words of Son-of-the-Star as Sitting Bear remembers hearing them.[1]

The beginning of the permanent friendship between the Arikara and the whites came about from a meeting held by *Grand-father,* as they called him, on Mussel Shell River in Montana. There was one representative of the Arikara tribe at this meeting, Bear Chief, and he was given authority to choose a colleague on his return, to be chief with him over the Arikara. White Shield was so named and he afterwards appointed Son-of-the-Star as head of the Arikara police. Each chief, according to Arikara custom, had such a police force. The purpose of the Mussel Shell meeting was peace. And thus the police were to prevent hostilities between the Arikara and the whites. The whole camp was full

---

[1] Unless otherwise stated the regular interpreter of these narratives was Peter Beauchamp, a graduate of Hampton Institute, Virginia. The numerous footnotes that accompany this narrative are added to indicate how closely the Indian story agrees with the general trend of the official and unofficial accounts of the same events.

of respect for the new regime of order and peace, even the oldest of the tribe. The police served to check inter-tribal skirmishes, but not all of the tribes respected the new plan, for the Dakotas continued to plague the Arikara. At this time there were many whites spread far and wide, working in wood camps, on boats, etc., and the Dakotas massacred them. The Arikara and the whites suffered the same fate. This continued from bad to worse; some of the Arikara present at this meeting had helped to defend the whites against the Dakotas. Now Bear Chief died and White Shield was still living when Son-of-the-Star was called to Washington because of his services as chief of police. Son-of-the-Star took with him to Washington, Bull Head, Peter Beauchamp, the interpreter, and three Mandans, Bad Gun, Bald Eagle, and Chief Red Cow's son, Show-Fear-in-the-Face (the one older than Black Eagle). This was about the year 1874.[2] When they arrived at Washington the Indian commissioner greeted Son-of-the-Star. He began the council with these words: "Son-of-the-Star, I have sent for you because I wish to see you. Now I see you for you stand before me. Son-of-the-Star, you have seen me with your own eyes. What is your

[2] In 1875, a year before Custer's Big Horn fight, the following Indians went to Washington: Bad Gun, Dance-Flag, and Running Face, Mandans, the interpreter being Chas. Packenau; Son-of-Star, Bull Head, and Black Fox, Arikara, with their interpreter, Peter Beauchamp.— *Collections of the State Historical Society of North Dakota*, Bismarck, 1908 II, p. 466.

opinion of me?" Son-of-the-Star replied: "Yes,
I have seen you, I admire you, I admire your whole
being. We can depend upon you for protection, we
have faith that you will protect us. I came at your
call because I felt weak. We have kept our promise,
we have kept peace. We have tried to protect the
whites among us. I see myself that I am weak.
You are strong, whatever you need you have ready.
You have all that is needed to protect yourselves in
the way of weapons. I feel that in comparison
with you I am as a little child dodging the blows of
someone stronger. To consult with you about this
is my one purpose in coming to you. My game and
my means for providing for my people have been
diminished. It is all the same, you have cattle and
you have provisions." The commissioner said:
"Son-of-the-Star, you have touched my heart. I
am sorry that both your people and mine have
trouble with the Dakotas. You have made tears
come to my eyes. Yes, Son-of-the-Star, I have a
great many boys (soldiers). I will do what you
suggest. I will decide to fight Sitting Bull and I
will fight him. It will not be ten years, it will probably be two or three years, if Sitting Bull is strong.
But if you look around the earth you will see clouds
of dust going up to the sky where my armies are setting out after Sitting Bull. Sitting Bull is like a
prisoner in a room, four walls shut him in, he cannot escape. I have my boys all around him. If he
breaks one circle there will be another around him.

He cannot escape, he has no way of going under the earth, and no way of getting away from me. It will probably be about two years after you arrive home that the expedition against Sitting Bull will set out. Son-of-the-Star, you will furnish some boys for this expedition." Son-of-the-Star replied: "Yes, I have boys (warriors), they will take part in the expedition." Then he asked the commissioner what the plan would be if his boys were to help on the expedition. The reply was: "If I lose one of your boys, he or his relatives will have money for a long time. In the event that one of the boys is wounded, I will reward him. While the boys are under me, doing any work for the government, should they be injured accidentally in storm, in flood, or by breaking a leg or arm, or by any other accident in service, I will remember that he is under my orders and that he is entitled to a reward. The boys that work in the service shall be rewarded, if they are wounded about the eyes or head, their injuries shall be paid for. I will remember that I am responsible for them and reward them also, for any loss of stock or horses." Son-of-the-Star replied that he would comply with the wishes of the commissioner. The commissioner then went into another room and brought out a Winchester rifle for each of them and gave it to them. He said: "Any time I issue goods to you, I will also send guns. I will try and make you happy. I will provide you with provisions, I will provide you with cattle. After the Sioux have been broken up, you will probably be visited by straggling Sioux who have no longer any land. I want you to treat them well and share what you have with them. Think of them as prisoners, those taken by the soldiers and held in captivity." Two years after Son-of-the-Star's arrival home, he received a letter from the Indian commissioner asking him to carry out his promise. A council was called to take the matter into consideration, and Sitting Bear said, "Those here tonight volunteered to go, though some of them were very young. This is what we consider an agreement between the United States Government and ourselves."

Story of the First Enlistment of the Arikara as United States Scouts. (Told by Sitting Bear, who spoke in place of Soldier.)

The first time I heard of the Arikara enlistment was when the steamboat first arrived at Fort Berthold. We were told that this boat had on it three United States representatives. It was announced that a council was to be held by these representatives with the three tribes. At this time there were many honored men alive among the three tribes. In Fort Berthold village there was a large Arikara medicine-lodge and here the representatives of the three tribes met with those representatives from the United States. They asked the United States representatives what was wanted of them. The first speaker said that they had come to obtain consent of the three tribes to have a portion of their reservation ceded to the United States. He told them that this request was made in order to have an establishment there where the United States authorities could look out for them. The representatives of the three tribes formally approved of the plan. They agreed to give up land as follows: Beginning at the mouth of Snake Creek and going northeast to Dog Den Butte, from thence east to Corn Cob Buttes, thence south to the old Arikara Village at Fort Clark, thence up the Missouri River on the west side to the point of starting. While this was under the consideration of the council no objection was raised to it; the area, price, etc., were not taken up as yet. The Arikara representatives were White Shield, Son-of-the-Star, Iron Bear (Shows-fear-in-the-face), and Black Road (Trail).

White Shield spoke first for the Arikara, Crow Gizzard (Crow's Breast), Hidatsa chief, spoke second, Red Cow, for the Mandans, spoke third. The interpreter for all three tribes was Pierre Garreau. Before the business was completed, and while the discussion was still going on, an alarm came of a Dakota attack on the village. All the Indians left the lodge and the United States representatives were left alone. It was reported that while the fight was going on one of these commissioners went up on the lodge with a paper and prayed for victory for the three tribes. They were victorious and killed five Dakotas, one of whom wore a war-bonnet. Thus the United States representatives were eye-witnesses of our difficulties and troubles. Not all of the Indians went out to fight, a few of the old people remained in the lodge and we do not know what happened there. When we came back the steamboat that had brought the United States representatives had gone, for the fight had lasted all day. It was very hot and some horses died of heat. The Dakotas were chased from Timber Coulee to Blue Hills near Rose Glen. I do not know how many Indian representatives stayed behind in the tepee, but White Shield and Son-of-the-Star stayed and they told the rest of the Indians about the prayer of the white man and Pierre Garreau also told them that this man had prayed. The white man when he prayed had a book or paper in his hand. The Indians had been so successful in the fight that they looked upon the praying white man as a holy man. Summer went, fall came, the soldiers came on the steamboat and located the fort (Stevenson) up the river from the land agreed upon. When the three tribes heard of this some of their representatives went down to see the officer at Fort Stevenson about the location of the fort on land not granted in the treaty. This was while the soldiers were still living in tents. The buildings were not up. At this conference the officer replied that they had located the fort nearer to the three tribes in order to help them better, but that the land upon which Fort Stevenson was built still belonged to

the Indians (Sitting Bear did not know this, or
what was said, by being present at the conference,
but reported only what he heard). The following
spring permanent building began. The officer in
charge asked F. F. Gerard to arrange with the Arikara to come down to Fort Stevenson and enlist as
scouts, and he particularly named Bull Head. Gerard was at Fort Stevenson at this time, as trader
or clerk, and he likely suggested Bull Head to the
officer in charge. All the Arikara who responded
to Gerard's call were members of the police force
of White Shield. Red Dog and Tall Bear were at
Fort Stevenson at this time visiting Gerard and he
said to them: "I am glad to see you for I have an
order for enlistment of Arikara scouts. I will send
by you this hard tack, bacon, coffee, sugar, and
front quarter of beef. You take it all back to Fort
Berthold and make a feast and help me enlist." So
Red Dog and Tall Bear took the provisions back on
their horses to the village. It was after dark when
they got back. "I was in bed when Red Dog opened
my door and said I was to meet at Tall Bear's to see
about enlistment." Gerard, he said, had given him
provisions, and had particularly named Soldier and
Two Bears as being the ones he wanted. (The
above quotation is in Soldier's own words.) Soldier
went with Red Dog to the lodge of Tall Bear. Besides these two there were present in his lodge the
following: Big Star, Dog's Backbone, White Ghost
(Smoke), Ree Chief, Elk Head (Not-Afraid-of-

Anybody), Bull Head, Red Elk, Charging Bull, Two Bears, Tall Bear, Only Brave, and Peter Beauchamp. These fourteen people were all who were present. Tall Bear and Red Dog opened the meeting and told them why they had called them together. They said they had been at Fort Stevenson and that Gerard had given them some provisions. Now, as members of White Shield's police force, they suggested that they all go down and enlist. "We will fare like other soldiers," they said, "food, pay, and lodging, and we go with this understanding." They voted one by one to go until all agreed. The next day they packed up and went to Fort Stevenson, some on foot, others on horseback. They had knives, bows and arrows, and only Indian dress. At Fort Stevenson Gerard met them and told them to camp. He gave them rations and said that the officer would see them next day. They camped in tents supplied to them, across on the other side of Garrison Creek. The next day they went up to the officer's house and were told to come in. They all stripped to the breech clout and were examined by the army doctor, for only strong men were wanted for the hard work. After inspection they received complete suits of clothes, each a hat with a feather, under-clothes, flannel shirt, shoes, and a blue cape. Here they received also long, breech-loading rifles with three brass bands (the interpreter added at this point that he had heard these were 45-70's). Soon these guns were exchanged for shorter ones (about three and one-half feet long), cavalry guns with magazines holding seven cartridges. They received also cartridge belts and bags for extra shells. They were given one horse for their camp and they took turns using it.

The Narrative as continued by Soldier.

Bull Head was made head of the band by the officer; he had three stripes on his arm and black trouser stripes. On his hat he wore a brass bugle emblem. Bull Head detailed Two Bears and Soldier to look after the rations furnished. The ration consisted of square thick crackers, salt, fresh bread, flour, bacon, sugar, plug tobacco, tea, beans, peas, hominy, and square, solid strips of beans and leaves mixed (succotash), and occasionally fresh beef. They boiled the succotash, it seemed to be a mixture of cabbage leaves and beans. They were furnished with tin plates, large cups, kettles, and a camp stove or oven. For pay each man received sixteen dollars per month and for each horse twelve dollars extra. They were paid every two months. "What first took the heart out of my body (made it jump with happiness) was the sight of the green paper money in my hands." Soldier served six winters at Fort Stevenson, enlisting for six months at a time. For this reason he took no part in the village battles against the Dakotas as did so many others and he has nothing to tell of them. He said, "I was once working in the woods when I heard a war-cry that

the Sioux had carried off the horses." He rushed
out, got on a horse, and met Peter Beauchamp carrying a quiver and a rifle. They rode across a hill
and they saw two Dakota warriors on a ridge ahead.
Soldier told Beauchamp to make ready and be brave
in the fight, for Beauchamp was still untried in war.
Beauchamp got out of patience at his insistence and
replied: "I know what is coming, the birds and un-
derground people are hungry and if I am killed
they will feed on me, they will get fat on me, that is
what I expect." Then Beauchamp saw that he had
lost his bow, though he still had his quiver full of
arrows and his gun. The Dakotas retreated and
the Arikara could not overtake them for the enemy's horses were swifter. The other scouts tried to
head the Dakotas off, but Sitting Bull's band appeared and drove all the scouts in. Sitting Bull had
captured some boat loads of people on the river, but
he let them go and dashed out to attack the fort.
Bull Head was thrown from his horse and lay still
in the grass. Soldier swung around on the Dakotas
and was about to fire at them but Two Chiefs called
out to him not to fire. Two Dakota warriors rode
up and stood one on each side of the body of Bull
Head, as he lay stunned. One of them called out:
"I am Sitting Bull, himself." And he and his companion kept the rest of the Dakotas off from Bull
Head so that they did not hurt him. The scouts left
Bull Head lying and the Dakotas stripped him and
took his arms but did not hurt him because of Sit-

ting Bull and his companion. Then the white soldiers took a wagon out to bring back Bull Head's
body and Soldier saw someone coming in over the
hill, staggering, hardly able to walk; it was Bull
Head. Sitting Bull and Bull Head belonged to the
same secret society, the New Dog, and so Bull Head
was not hurt by the enemy.

The enlistment of the present Arikara Scouts as told by Young Hawk

Young Hawk's father enlisted first at Fort Lincoln and he himself stayed there with his father
and after a time his father suggested that he enlist
and earn money too. So he enlisted under Lieutenant Gurley at Fort Lincoln. At this time an army
of cavalry came there under Custer from the West.[3]
Fort Lincoln was then on top of the hill but Custer
changed the camp to the bottom land and scouts
were put under his command.

Custer then set out on the Black Hills expedition
and Young Hawk accompanied him. We were
told that this expedition was for the purpose of lo-

[3] Lieutenant General Sheridan of the Military Division of the Missouri refers to this event in his report of October 27, 1873, as follows:
''Early last spring in consequence of reported attacks by the Indians
on the post of Fort Abraham Lincoln, I deemed it necessary that a
regiment of cavalry should be transferred to the Department of Dakota
in order that these Indians might be followed and punished, if they
again renewed their attacks. On application to headquarters of the army
the Seventh Cavalry was ordered from the Military Division of the South
to the Department of Dakota, and by direction of Gen. A. H. Terry,
stationed at Forts Rice and Abraham Lincoln.''— *Report of the Secretary
of War, 1873-1874*, Wash., 1874, I, p. 40.

cating gold. We saw men in the party who were surveyors with instruments and they used them on the hills and streams.[4] Some time after the arrival of the expedition at Black Hills, Custer came up with something concealed in his hands. Then Custer put a yellow nugget in Young Hawk's hand and it felt very heavy.[5] He was told it was gold and the scouts were told to look for more of it, and they did on their hands and knees.[6] The timber was heavy and much delay was caused in preparing roads through it. The timber continued heavy until Custer was discouraged. The scouts climbed high hills and saw more timber. Then Custer called for someone to go ahead and see what was beyond. He called Young Hawk and gave him a compass to find his way with and at last Custer ordered some scouts to go with Charley Reynolds to the Mussel Shell River. The scouts who were sent on this expedition were Rough Horn, Bear's Ears, Red Bear, Young Hawk, Strikes Two, Bloody Knife, and Red Horse.

[4] Captain William Ludlow, chief engineer of the Department of Dakota, and his assistants of the Engineer Battalion made daily instrumental observations, in taking the general topography and locating important elevations with the transit, preparatory to making maps of the country.— Ludlow, *Report of a Reconnaissance of the Hills of Dakota*, Wash., 1875, pp. 7, 13, 16.

[5] The gold excitement with regard to the Black Hills which furnished one of the motives for the expedition of 1874, had this origin. Some Indians brought some small grains and nuggets of gold into a frontier trading-post. Whiskey and presents induced them to disclose that these came from the Black Hills.— Dodge, Lieut. Col. R. I., *The Black Hills*, N. Y., 1876, pp. 9-10.

[6] See *Appendix*, 130.

A company of cavalry went along and after two days and nights they came out of the timber and Charley Reynolds said: "The distance is short." After reaching Mussel Shell River they returned to Custer. The army followed the scouts and came out at Bear Butte and so went back to Fort Lincoln.

At the same time that Young Hawk enlisted, thirty other Arikara enlisted also, as follows: Strikes Two, Red Bear, Little Sioux, Enemy Heart, Standing Soldier, Horns-in-Front (Young Hawk's father), Growling Bear (Bear Growls), Rough Horn, Bull Neck, Pretty Wolf, Dry Bear (Very Lean Bear), Bear's Eye (second name, Wolf-Stands-in-the Cold), Foolish Bear, Black Rabbit, Angry Bear, Charging Bull, Goose, Paint, Left Handed, String Ear-rings, Crow Bear, Angry Bull, Sees-the-Track, Carries-the-Moccasin-about-the-Room, Bear Robe, Bear's Ears, Bull-in-the-Water, Bear's Belly, Two Bulls, and Pointed Hill. After the camp had moved down on the flat, White Belly enlisted. By the time Young Hawk returned his period of enlistment was up and he went back to Fort Berthold with most of the scouts.

The Second Enlistment, as told by Young Hawk.

General Custer had told them that he was going on another expedition and that they might be called upon to serve. After his return Young Hawk decided not to serve any more, but his father insisted that he should go. After a time Son-of-the-Star

got a letter from Custer asking for more scouts. It
was announced that Son-of-the-Star would call a
council in his own house and many came. Son-of-
the-Star said: "My boys, I have had a letter from
a white man asking for some of you boys to serve
as scouts." He told them that they would serve
under Long Hair (Custer) and they were not surprised at this, for they had heard him say he would
go on another expedition, and, besides, Son-of-the-
Star had been to Washington.[7] His words were
heard by all present and all that was necessary to
say was: "I will go." Young Hawk's father said,
"I will go and my son, too." Those who promised
to go at this time and afterwards enlisted were:
Bob-tailed Bull, Stabbed, Charging Bull, Horns-in-
Front, Young Hawk, Bull-in-the-Water, Little
Brave, Bloody Knife, Tall Bear (High Bear), One
Feather, Running Wolf, Red Star, Strikes Two,
Foolish Bear, Howling Wolf, White Eagle, Crook-
ed Horn, Strikes-the-Lodge, Scabby Wolf, Pretty
Face, Curly Head (Hair), Black Fox, and One
Horn. Certain scouts had reënlisted at Fort Lin-
coln and were already in service. Red Bear was
asked to remain by Crooked Horn, so that they
could return to Fort Lincoln together and he did so.
Red Bear spent the winter at Heart Camp, two
miles up from Armstrong and the next winter Wolf-
Stands-in-the-Cold came up from Fort Lincoln

---

[7] General Custer had for a long time been called "Ouches" or Long
Hair, by the Indians. — Mrs. Elizabeth Custer, *Boots and Saddles*, 190.

with word that additional scouts were needed. He
was seen by Red Bear when he arrived.

Red Bear's Story.

I did not know they had called a council to see
who would volunteer. I knew they were enlisting
when Boy Chief, my brother, asked me for a horse
so that he could go and be a scout. I was away from
the camp at the time of both meetings. Boy Chief,
with some of his young friends, started for Fort
Lincoln a few days before Son-of-the-Star asked
for volunteers. My brother and the rest had been
gone three or four days when I went to the agency
office and saw Son-of-the-Star, who said: "I see you
have not gone." I hadn't thought of going and this
touched my pride, I thought it over. I remembered
my one brother had been killed in United States
service but I decided to follow with the rest. Son-
of-the-Star said: "I am glad you wish to go and I
want you to be brave." Then Son-of-the-Star asked
for a passport for me and the agent gave it to me.
I went as soon as I could find my horses. Only
Brave went with me, we had our wives. Only Brave
was going to visit not to enlist. We were two days
on the road, we crossed on the ferry at Bismarck
and when I arrived at Fort Lincoln I noticed the
scout quarters west of the post. I stopped at the
tent of Wolf-Standing-in-the-Cold, who was married to my sister. I knew my sister was there so I
went where she was. The scouts already enlisted

then were: Soldier, Strikes Two, Little Brave, Left-Handed, Red Foolish Bear, Running Wolf, Red Wolf, Little Sioux, Boy Chief, Bull, Cha-ra-ta (Mandan name), Black Porcupine, Goose. These were the men to go on the expedition with Custer to the west. There were there two young Arikara, Owl and Wagon, who were not enlisted. Red Bear showed his permit to Gerard who said: "There are two boys here, get them with you to enlist when you enlist," meaning Owl and Wagon. Gerard took them all over to the office of the commanding officer and he took in Red Bear's permit and coming out soon told them they were to enlist and get clothes and arms. After medical examination was over, Gerard took them into Custer's office where Custer's brother (Tom, the one with the scar on his face) was. He raised his hand and Gerard told the Indians to raise theirs also. Custer soon came in and told them through Gerard that they were the last scouts to enlist and for that reason, since the expedition was ready, they must remain on duty at Fort Lincoln.

Boy Chief's Story of His Enlistment.

Bob-tailed Bull found Boy Chief at Fort Berthold village and told him some of the boys were going to enlist as scouts at Fort Lincoln. Again a little later Bob-tailed Bull saw him and told him that the boys had started for Fort Lincoln. So Boy Chief got a horse, saddled up, and started last of all.

He caught up with them just out of the Bad Lands,
as they sat smoking. As he came up he saw there
Son-of-the-Star, Peter Beauchamp, Bob-Tailed
Bull, Shoots-at-the-Bear, Big Star, Growling Bear,
and others he cannot recall. They stopped over
night at Fort Stevenson. About where Hancock is
the ice began to break up. At three miles below the
house of old Joe Taylor there was a building where
the army mail carriers exchanged mail (the Arikara
call it Porcupine Dens). They stopped there that
night, and a hard snow and rain storm came on but
they were comfortable there. They waited two days,
and by the third day they were not only out of provisions but also very hungry. The storm had lasted
all this time. They could do nothing but wait. Son-
of-the-Star and Beauchamp went to the man in
charge of the mail house and told him they were out
of provisions and very hungry, and that they were
on their way to enlist at Fort Lincoln. This man
was willing to feed them, he baked a dish pan full
of bread and gave it to them with coffee, saying he
had little himself but he could do this much for
them. The next morning, the 4th, it was clear and
they set out for the crossing near Bismarck. Late
in the evening they came to Bismarck, the end of
the railroad. There were several buildings there
with soldiers and Beauchamp and Son-of-the-Star
had a talk with the officer. The soldiers were about
to cross the river and the Indians were told to hold
up their right hands. Then they were all taken into

quarters. Apparently it was too late for supper, and though they were very hungry, they got nothing, though their horses were fed well. Taps called them to bed very hungry. The bugle called them out of bed in the morning and they ate a big breakfast, sitting a long time at the table. They were given feed and hay for their horses. The ferry was out of order and they were delayed there seven days. During this time they lived with the soldiers all the time and were fed well. On the seventh day (which was probably Sunday), just at dark, they were warned to be ready in the morning. The next day they went over on the ferry and got to Fort Lincoln, which was down on the flat. Bob-Tailed Bull took him to headquarters to "touch the pen" (enlistment papers). He thought that the medical examination would throw him out, as he was very young, but he passed. In another room an officer enlisted him, and they received guns at another building, and at another, clothing and two gray blankets apiece.

Soldier's Account of an Interview with Custer.

Soldier and Bob-tailed Bull met Custer at his camp on the river bank, in his own tent, Gerard was interpreter. Custer said: "The man before me, Bob-tailed Bull, is a man of good heart, of good character. I am pleased to have him here. I am glad he has enlisted. It will be a hard expedition but we will all share the same hardships. I am very

well pleased to have him in my party, and I told it
at Washington. We are to live and fight together,
children of one father and one mother. The great-
grandfather has a plan. The Sioux camps have
united and you and I must work together for the
Great Father and help each other. The Great Father is well pleased that it was so easy (took few
words) to get (coax) Son-of-the-Star to furnish me
scouts for this work we have to do and he is pleased,
too, at his behavior in helping on the plan of the
Great Father. I, for one, am willing to help in this
all I can, and you must help too. It is this way, my
brothers. If I should happen to lose any of the
men Son-of-the-Star has furnished, their reward
will not be forgotten by the government. Their re-
lations will be saddened by their death but there
will be some comfort in the pay that the United
States government will provide."

Bob-tailed Bull replied: "It is a good thing you
say, my brother, my children and other relatives
will receive my pay and other rewards. I am glad
you say this for I see there is some gain even though
I lose my life."

Custer then said: "No more words need be said.
Bob-tailed Bull is to be leader and Soldier second
in command of the scouts."

Clothing was issued to the two leaders, on Bob-
tailed Bull's sleeve there were three stripes, and on
Soldier's sleeve there were two. Custer called on
Bob-tailed Bull to speak, and he said through Ge-

rard, that he was not a man to change tribes all the time, that he was always an Arikara and respected their chiefs and had served under them gladly. He said: "Yes, Long Hair, I am a member of the police and also chief, with one hand I hold the position of police among my people and with the other I hold the position of chief of the scouts. My brother, I am going to address you so, for you said we were brothers, I have had experience fighting the Sioux, and when we meet them we shall see each other's bravery."

Red Star's Story of the March from Fort Lincoln to Powder River.

There was no Indian ceremony at Fort Lincoln before the march, but on the way to Fort Lincoln they sang their war songs at every camp. We were all waiting six days, Custer had gone east to Washington.[8] Red Star heard of his return and there

8 General Custer had received peremptory telegraphic summons to Washington, about March 16, 1876, to testify before a Congressional committee with regard to alleged abuses of the War Department in connection with the post-trader business. A provision of a military bill, of 1870, gave the secretary of war power to appoint traders at the military posts on the frontier, and this investigation concerned an alleged sale by Secretary Belknap of a post-tradership to a person called Marsh. Belknap had resigned his office under charges and was at once impeached by the House of Representatives. In St. Paul, on his way home to Fort Lincoln, Custer was notified May 5th by telegram that he was not to accompany the expedition against the Indians. When this expedition was planned by Sheridan and Sherman it was ordered that Custer should be assigned to the command of the Dakota column. Custer's appeal to the president for permission to be allowed to go with his regiment was supported by Brigadier General Terry, the department

was a rumor of a call to meet Custer at Fort Lincoln, the regular headquarters, but he is not certain of such a meeting. Bob-tailed Bull, Bloody Knife, Tall Bear, Stabbed, Black Fox, and Crooked Horn went to meet Custer. Not one of the present scouts attended this meeting with Custer at headquarters but he heard that Custer was well pleased with the appearance of the scouts. Custer was happy to see Bloody Knife, he presented him with a handkerchief and a medal, which were given to him for Bloody Knife at Washington.[9] Then he recognized one of his old scouts, Black Fox. "If he repeats his trick of the last time," he said, "I will have a remedy, if he takes his wife along again he will be well punished." Custer was pleased to see the beautifully decorated shirt which belonged to Bob-tailed Bull. Custer told him that he had been to Washington and that he had been informed that this would be his last campaign in the West among the Indians. He said that no matter how small a victory he could win, even though it were against only five tents of Dakotas, it would make him President, Great Father, and he must turn back as soon as he was victo-

commander. The President yielded to these petitions and permitted Custer to go with the expedition as lieutenant colonel of his regiment. Custer had hoped to take the field early in April. It was May 7th by the time he received the answer to his request. — Whittaker, *Life of Gen. Geo. A. Custer*, N. Y., 1876, pp. 535-562; J. E. Walker, *Campaigns of Gen. Custer*, N. Y., 1881, pp. 40-47.

[9] General Custer valued Bloody Knife, his favorite Indian scout, for his splendid service during the Black Hills expedition of 1874. He had proved himself an invaluable and faithful scout. — Mrs. Elizabeth Custer, *Boots and Saddles*, 302.

rious. In case of victory he would take Bloody Knife back with him to Washington.

It was early in the morning when the bugle sounded, and the camp broke up and the march began. The army strung out in order toward the fort. Gerard told the scouts they were to have their own company, and they were the first to parade on the fort grounds.[10] He told them to form themselves by societies in order, first the New Dog Society (the oldest men in it), second the Grass Dance Society, and third the Da-roch-pa (its members had a crescent moon shaved on the back of head). At the head of the New Dog Society were Soldier and Crooked Horn. The Grass Dance leaders were Young Hawk and Bob-tailed Bull. The leaders of the Da-roch'-pa were Strikes-the-Lodge and Bull-Stands-in-the-Water. The parade ended and the march began, with Custer ahead. There were four Dakota scouts who had been at Fort Lincoln that went along with the Arikara. One of these scouts was Ca-roó, another was Ma-tōk'-sha, a third was Mach-pē'-as-ka (White Cloud), the fourth was Ptä-ä'-tĕ (Buffalo Ancestor). The first camp was on both sides of the Heart River.[11] A drove of cattle went along to

---

10 By 7 o'clock on May 17th, the Seventh Cavalry was marching around the parade-ground of Fort Lincoln led by the band playing "Garry Owen," the battle tune of the Seventh. General Terry had consented to this demonstration, or perhaps ordered it, in order that the formidable appearance the command presented might allay the fears of those left behind. — Capt. E. S. Godfrey, *Custer's Last Battle, Century,* 1892, p. 358.

11 Brig. Gen. E. S. Godfrey states that the command struck straight

furnish beef to the soldiers; he saw them on the first day's march. The white soldiers were paid off at this camp, the scouts did not receive any pay at all for they were just enlisted.[12] The second camp was at a place called Stone House, north of Heart River but in sight of its timber. The third camp was made where a hail storm struck the line of march; it was about time to stop for the day.[13] The fourth camp was on a hill, and here they had a hard thunder storm, the lightning struck in the middle of the camp. The scouts saw the soldiers looking at the place where it struck. At this camp Red Star, Bull-in-the-Water, and Strikes-the-Lodge were detailed for scout duty. The fifth camp was at a place near Young Maiden's Breasts (Buttes), we passed these hills and camped a little beyond, a little north of what is now the line of the Northern Pacific Railway.[14] The sixth camp was a little east of the

across the country from the old post on the hill to the first camp on the Heart River.— Letter of Brig. Gen. E. S. Godfrey, May, 1912.

The scouts on being questioned at a later meeting said that Custer's wife and sister were not seen the first day's march. At the first camp Custer's wife arrived. On the first day's march the Arikara scouts marched in the rear of Custer's command but they do not know why.

[12] The troops were paid off at the Heart River camp by Major Wm. Smith, later paymaster general. — Letter of Brig. Gen. E. S. Godfrey, May, 1912, 1-2. Mrs. Elizabeth Custer, *Boots and Saddles*, p. 265.

[13] General Terry in his report to Sheridan had the following to say about the first days of the march: ''This column marched on the morning of May 17th. For some days its progress was slow, for the wagons were heavily laden and recent rains had made the ground extremely soft.''— *Report of Secretary of War for 1876*, Wash., 1876, I, p. 460.

[14] ''In general we paralleled the N. P. routing, keeping to the mesa or plateau because of the soft ground in the valleys, keeping north of

present town of Hebron, in some groves of box elder. All this time Custer was always first on the march.[15] They passed the site of what is now Hebron and marched on to the hills near by. Breakfast was always ready just after daybreak each day of the march. The seventh camp was at Young Man's Butte.[16] Custer picked out his own camps because he knew the country well.[17] The scouts were kept in details on the flank and on the hills ahead all night. There was plenty of game. Strikes Two was a very good old hunter and Young Hawk was a good young hunter. The scouts always camped near Custer's headquarters, and as they were getting supper Custer came to them on a visit. They knew his choice of meat very well and how he liked to have it cooked. Young Hawk always cooked his meat for him, and Custer was very fond of him, and also of Goose because they were jolly young fellows, reckless and full of life. Custer said to them by signs that he liked to see men eat meat by the fire; if they were full, they would be strong.

the N. P. till we got to the Bad Lands of the Little Missouri.''—Letter of Brig. Gen. E. S. Godfrey, May, 1912, p. 2.

15 This was customary on Custer's expeditions. His zeal is best described by his own words in connection with the Black Hills expedition, ''I have attempted to be several other things besides commanding officer, particularly guide since the expedition started.''—Mrs. Elizabeth Custer, *Boots and Saddles*, p. 304.

16 ''One of our camps was at 'Young Men's Butte,' at the head of the Knife River.''—Letter of Brig. Gen. E. S. Godfrey, May, 1912, 2.

17 Two years before Custer had passed through this country. The trail of the Black Hills Expedition of 1874 was practically followed to the Black Hills. — *Ib.*, p. 2.

Once Custer was eating with them when he said through Gerard, the interpreter: "There is one thing I do not like, there are three tribes of you and only one represented here tonight. It was agreed that they should all be represented." He said he had made up his mind to go on this expedition to fight. He said he had been to Washington and had been given instructions to follow the Dakotas. Now that he was on the war-path, if he had a victory, he said: "When we return, I will go back to Washington, and on my trip to Washington I shall take my brother here, Bloody Knife, with me. I shall remain at Washington and be the Great Father. But my brother, Bloody Knife, will return, and when he arrives home he shall have a fine house built for him, and those of you present will be the ones appointed to look after the work that will be placed in charge of Bloody Knife. You will have positions under him to help in what he is to do and you can, when you wish to speak with me or send me word, gather at Bloody Knife's house and decide what the message will be. Then he will send it to me. He will be given the whole tribe of the Arikara to be the head of. I will have papers made out for each of you here, then you will have plenty to eat for all time to come, and you and your children."

Custer continued: "When these papers are in your hands, you will have food to eat always. In case your child is hungry and wants something to eat, take your papers to any citizen and he will divide with you. Take them to any store, and when they are read, they will speak and tell what you wish and you will get it. You will be the ones after we return who will have charge of the Arikara tribe.'' He then asked if the Mandans and the Arikara were friends, and was told that they were. He did not ask if the Grosventre were friends of the Arikara.

He then continued: ''I don't like it because the Mandans and Grosventre are not here. While you are out on scout duty, you should see a party of Indians coming to visit us, and you find out that they are Grosventre, we will shoot them down and kill them. If one or more of this party that comes are Mandans, you will divide your provisions and ammunition with them, for they are probably hunting.''

Story of how the Mail was brought to Custer's Camp by Red Bear.

At Custer Camp No. 8, One Horn and Red Foolish Bear were sent back with mail to Fort Lincoln. John Howard was interpreter at Fort Lincoln in place of Gerard, and he told Red Bear to take One Horn's place and go to Custer's camp. Red Bear had been retained at this post because his mare was unable to travel. This was at sundown, and they were to report at dark at headquarters. The mail would then be ready for them, and they were to

start with it at once. When the wives of the Arikara
scouts heard that these two were going to join Custer they began to bring in moccasins for their hus-
bands at Custer's camp, very many pairs of moccasins. They went over with Howard to headquarters for the mail. There were some soldiers there
and they brought out a large sack of mail. Red
Bear wondered about his poor horse with this mail
and all the moccasins, but Red Foolish Bear's load
was the same. Howard said he would go part of the
way with them. He went a little way, then said
good-bye and rode back. They reached Heart
River, unsaddled, and slept a little. At daybreak
they started again, cutting straight across to Young
Maiden's Buttes. In the afternoon they were hungry. Red Bear had some crackers and lump sugar
which his wife had put into his bullet pouch. These
he divided with Red Foolish Bear. Then his horse
began to give out. Food was short, he tried to shoot
an antelope but missed twice. Red Foolish Bear
was better mounted and got ahead. Red Bear
walked most of the way, and could hardly keep up
with his companion. They talked over how much
longer his mare could keep up. They chose a camp
in a ravine that had a little stagnant water. Red
Bear unsaddled his mare and turned her loose. She
was very tired and lay down instantly. They saw a
jack rabbit, and Red Foolish Bear shot it for supper, and they roasted it there. They crossed the
trail of the army beyond the Young Maiden's

Buttes and made supper on what they found thrown away on the march. Red Bear proposed to his companion that he go ahead on his good horse, but he refused. They found plenty of food along the trail which the soldiers had thrown away. The next day they made Bull Snake Camp. Red Foolish Bear insisted on staying with Red Bear though the army was getting farther away every day. At sunset they smoked together, and then Red Foolish Bear said good-bye and galloped off, telling Red Bear he would follow the trail all the way. Beyond the present site of Dickinson Red Bear found the road very difficult and his mare lay down for rest as soon as she was unsaddled. Red Foolish Bear got into camp that night, but the scouts did not come back for Red Bear for fear of frightening him. At sunrise he saddled up and went on. Then he saw some Indians coming, and he thought they were Dakotas, and made ready to fight on a little hill. Then he saw Bob-tailed Bull leading the scouts, and he said to Red Bear: "This is a hard trip you have had, this is a soldier's life, you cannot get away from your duty. There is a horse being brought for you and your breakfast."

Red Wolf and Scabby Wolf then came up; there were six in all. They told him that there was no need to hurry, as the army would not march until noon. Red Bear went to headquarters where he delivered the mail, there were many newspapers and letters. Custer told Red Bear through Gerard that a soldier's life was hard, and that it was difficult to carry the words of the Great Father. Custer then asked about his horse, and Red Bear said that he had abandoned it. Custer replied through Gerard: "I know you have lost a horse in the government service. If we return alive you can choose money or a horse in the place of the one you have lost." In their camp Strikes Two loaned him a big black horse to ride.

Continuation of Red Star's Story.

Camp 8 was made at a spot just beyond where Dickinson now stands. Camp No. 9 was in a small ravine. Two bull-snakes were killed here and Robert Jackson,[17a] a half-breed Blackfoot Indian, put one of them around each leg. From Camp No. 10 we went on to Camp No. 11. Here the scouts had a horse race between a horse owned by Stabbed (the winner) and one owned by Pta-á-te. Each side put up ten dollars. We now went into the Bad Lands and some of the soldiers were set to making roads in the worst places.[18] Camp No. 12 was at the Little Missouri and Custer here forbade all shooting lest it should give warning to the Dakotas.[19] Rob-

---

[17a] Gerard calls him Wm. Jackson.

[18] "In going thru the Bad Lands we followed Sully's trail of 1864 down what was then known as Davis Creek and crossed the Little Missouri at 'Sentinel Butte' several miles above (south of) Medora the N. P. crossing; thereafter we were south of the N. P."—Letter of Brig. Gen. E. S. Godfrey, May, 1912, p. 2.

[19] On May 20th, in camp, forty-six miles from Fort Lincoln, General Custer wrote to Mrs. Custer as follows: "It is raining now, and has

ert Jackson shot his revolver at a snake in the river. The officer of the day came up and asked who had fired a shot and Jackson said, "I did it." They put him under discipline for this, a keg was turned upside down, and he stood on it on one foot. They now crossed the Little Missouri River to Soldier Hill (Sentinel Butte);[20] this was Camp No. 13.[21] Scabby Wolf and Left Handed were sent back to Fort Lincoln with mail and they later came back with the mail from Fort Lincoln.[22] Snow fell here, a heavy storm, some of the tents were drifted half way up to the top.[23] It cleared off very cold. They stayed here four sleeps and when they went

been since we started. The roads are fearfully bad. Here we are on the Little Muddy, after marching four days, and only forty-six miles from home. . . A wet season and bad roads can be looked for always in this region in the months of May and June."—Mrs. Elizabeth Custer, *Boots and Saddles*, pp. 304-305.

[20] On May 30th, Custer, with four companies of cavalry and some of the Arikara scouts, went on a fifty miles scout in the valley of the Little Missouri to determine the truth of the many rumors to the effect that the hostile Indians were gathering on the Little Missouri with the intention of fighting Custer's command there. In a letter to Mrs. Custer, dated this day he says: "Only think, we found the Little Missouri River so crooked and the Bad Lands so impassible that in marching fifty miles today we forded the river thirty-four (34) times." No Indians were found, nor evidence of their recent presence. — *Ib.*, pp. 305-307.

[21] This was May 31st. — *Report of Secretary of War, 1876*, I, p. 460.

[22] The General wrote to Mrs. Custer: "It has just been decided to send scouts back to Lincoln. They leave here at daylight, and will remain there thirty-six hours, returning to us with despatches and mail." — Mrs. Elizabeth Custer, *Boots and Saddles*, p. 305.

[23] On the 1st and 2d of June, the column was detained in camp by a heavy snow storm, on the edge of the Bad Lands which border the left bank of the Little Missouri. — *Report of Secretary of War, 1876*, I, .p 460.

on, they camped at Beaver Creek, Camp No. 14.[24]
Here scout Limping Grosventre came with mail
from the Yellowstone River. He told the scouts
that a soldier had been killed up there while hunting. They camped again on Beaver Creek, Camp
No. 15.[25] They march on to a coulee, the Dakota
scouts called it Cottonwood Creek, this was Camp
No. 16. They went on to a dry coulee with bunches
of willows. Here they could see the peaks of the
mountains by Powder River, this was Camp No.
17.[26] They marched towards the timber and when
they reached it they made Camp No. 18.[27] Here
two soldiers went out hunting and at dark they had
not returned. The scouts lighted fires for them on
the hills and they returned late at night. From
here they made a hurried march; they could now
see the bluffs on the Powder River. Custer ordered a halt and ordered that the cavalry only were
to go on. The infantry and wagon train were to
stay behind.[28] Then the order to move was sent

24 On the 3d of June, Beaver Creek was reached. — *Report of Secretary of War, 1876*, I, p. 460.

25 At Beaver Creek, the command turned south and followed that valley two days, June 4th to 6th, turning again to the west June 6th. — *Ib.*,
p. 461.

26 On the evening of June 7th, Powder River was reached at a point
about twenty miles from the Yellowstone. — *Ib.*

27 This was on the 9th.— Capt. E. S. Godfrey, *Custer's Last Battle*,
Century, January, 1892, p. 361.

28 General Terry went on June 8th to the mouth of the Powder River
to communicate with the supply steamer Far West. He went on the
steamer up the Yellowstone to meet General Gibbon. On his return he
ordered all the troops and supplies to be transferred to a depot to be

back to the scouts and they marched on the Powder River and made Camp No. 19.[29] Here Young Hawk, Forked Horn, One Feather, and the Dakota scout, Ca-roó, were detailed by Custer to follow up Powder River.

Young Hawk's Story of this Scouting Expedition.

These four Indians were sent ahead to scout for a detail of cavalry that followed after, two by two.[30] Custer ordered them to follow up Powder River and look for the Dakota trail. They were to go far up on one side and if they did not find the trail, they were to return on the other side in the same way. As soon as they struck the Dakota trail they were to instantly return to Custer. The party followed up the Powder River to the Tongue River and then went up the Tongue River. They got into the mountains and Young Hawk killed and cut up an elk which made him lose the rest of the party for

established at the mouth of the Powder River.— *Report of Secretary of War, 1876*, I, 461.

[29] This camp was reached June 10th. The General's letters to Mrs. Custer report that when the command was on the Powder River, it was in a country which had never been visited by white men; and they reveal how invaluable his services were as guide. Twice when he left the command it lost its way and Terry depended on Custer's gift in that line, again and again, to extricate the column in embarrassing situations. Mrs. Elizabeth Custer, *Boots and Saddles*, pp. 307-309.

The command remained in camp on the Powder River three days. Godfrey, *Custer's Last Battle*, p. 361.

[30] Major M. A. Reno started at 3 P.M., June 10th on a scout up the Powder River and to the Tongue River, to look for the trail of the Dakota. He found a heavy trail on the Tongue and followed it about forty miles up the Rosebud River. — *Ib.*, p. 362.

some time. He caught up with the rest of them on the Rosebud River and here fires were lighted. Forked Horn got the scouts out to go ahead and see what they could find. They saddled up and he told Young Hawk to go in a different direction from the rest. Young Hawk got on the hill where he could see the Rosebud River and discovered an abandoned camp with birds flying over it. It was a deserted Dakota camp and a horse was standing near it. He rode up to the deserted camp and saw evidence of many Indians having been there and he decided it was a Dakota camp. Saddles had been made here and the horses had trampled the bank at the watering place. He knew the camp was Dakota from what he could see of hide tanning, meat scaffolds, and the arrangement of tepees. Here the whole party camped, it was a very old camping place.[31] On the next day's scout they found an intrenchment showing evidence that all the white occupants had been killed. Our interpreter said this was the Bozeman party. The scouts found the camp by following the Dakota trail to it and they camped on the trail. The commanding officer of the cavalry called Forked Horn to him and said: "What do you think of this trail, Forked Horn?" Forked Horn replied: "If the Dakotas see us, the sun will not move very far before we are all killed. But you are leader and we will go on if you say

31 The trail seemed about three weeks old, and the number of lodges in the deserted village, estimated by the number of camp fires, were about 350. — Godfrey, *Custer's Last Battle*, pp. 362-363.

so.'' The commanding officer said: ''Custer told us to turn back if we found the trail, and we will return, these are our orders.'' They turned and followed the Rosebud River down to the Elk River and there they found Custer's camp. The cavalry only had come on. The infantry and wagon train stayed behind at Powder River.[32]

Red Star's Story, continued.

From Camp 19 we followed the Powder River down to the Yellowstone and made Camp No. 20.[33] Here was a large tent owned by a white man who was trading. The Arikara called him Arrow-Feathered-by-Crow-Feathers and he looked like an Arikara. This white trader was selling liquor to the soldiers.[34] The tent was black with soldiers buying liquor, it looked like a swarm of flies. There was no guardhouse at this camp and when the soldiers were arrested for being drunk they were taken out on the prairie and guarded there. The

32 All the wagons with their infantry guard were left at the depot at the mouth of the Powder River.— *Report of Secretary of War, 1876,* I., p. 461.

33 Camp No. 20 was made at the mouth of the Powder River, June 11th. As usual Custer was the guide; the company sent out the previous day to look for a road had lost its way but was found by the command at about 10 A.M. on the 11th. This camp was due west from Fort Lincoln.—Mrs. Elizabeth Custer, *Boots and Saddles,* p. 309.

34 The trader was James Coleman, who had come to the Powder River on the steamer Far West and had been put off for a few days to sell liquor. — For Coleman's story, see Appendix, p. 155.

The scouts all agreed that Custer took his hunting dogs as far as the Powder River camp. None of them saw the dogs after they rode back from the battle.

scouts were forbidden to drink for Gerard had told
them not to go to the tent. After a time when there
was less drinking and most of the white soldiers
had gone away, Gerard came to the scouts and told
them that Custer had permitted each one to buy
one drink. They had plenty of money for they had
killed game all the way on the march. The soldiers
bought the game at the following prices: deer's
hind quarter $2, front quarter $1, back or saddle
$1. (At this point Strikes Two interrupted the
interview and said that he had earned $200 this way
himself. Soldier said that his nephew, Goose,
hunted also and earned $128; he knew this because
he carried the purse. All of the scouts agreed that
they had made money this way and had plenty of
it at this camp.) Red Star spoke, also, and, in
confirmation of what the other scouts had just said,
related another instance.

At one of the earlier camps on Powder River, the
Da-roch-pa challenged the Grass Dancers to a Moccasin Game, and $300 was put up on each side. Two
white men, mule drivers of scout provision wagons,
took sides with the Indians, one on each side. The
Grass Dancers won the $600. They were two days
in camp here and there was a camp of soldiers just
across the river.[35] Two Arikara scouts were sent
out ahead, Stabbed and Goose, and they were given
a letter to take to the camp across the river. Here

[35] This was the camp of General Gibbon, with the Montana column,
who had been ordered by Terry to move eastward to meet him.— *Report
of Secretary of War, 1876,* I, p. 472.

there were some Crow scouts, and their interpreter, Man-with-a-Calfskin-Vest, came across the river to tell them about it. When Custer's army came up to Camp 20, Red Star saw the army across the river, it was already on the march up the Yellowstone.[36] Stabbed and Goose came back and reported to Custer's camp. Camp 20 was the base camp for the infantry, the band, all the wagons, and part of the mules. There was an inspection of the horses of the scouts and of the cavalry here.[37] Many had to stay behind because their horses were out of condition.[38] Those who stayed here were Red Bear,

[36] The column was on its way up the Yellowstone to the mouth of the Big Horn which it reached June 24th. There it was ferried across the Yellowstone by 4 A.M. before proceeding up the Little Big Horn. — *Report of Secretary of War, 1876*, I, pp. 473, 463.

[37] At the Powder River when Custer was inspecting the horses and forbidding those with disabled horses from going on with him, Howling Wolf hid his horse, thinking to evade the inspection. Custer asked Howling Wolf by signs where his horse was. Howling Wolf replied: "I put him on the island in the river, so he will be strong for the journey. He is as smooth and without galls as he was when he was a colt." Custer said impatiently: "Bring him here very quick or I will shoot him." Howling Wolf brought the horse and Custer said (here the narrator made a face which would resemble Custer's in such a case): "See that gall on his back, as large as my hand? What do you mean by your story?" Howling Wolf said to Custer: "You see the gall is behind the saddle. It is natural to him and was there when he was born. See, he is sound under the saddle. He can out-travel any horse but yours and should he fall I will keep up with you on foot." Custer laughed and said: "Since you are a wolf you may go." Howling Wolf had been riding for several days with the saddle far back so as to have his horse in good trim when they should meet the Dakotas.

[38] Reno told High Bear that he could not go with the rest because his horse was badly galled. High Bear said to him: "You see the sun there, if you say it does not move I will not dispute you." This is the polite way the Indians have of telling any one that his opinion is totally

Tall Bear, Horns-in-Front, Cha-rá-ta, Foolish Bear
(Crooked Foot), Running Wolf, Howling Wolf,
Curly Head. Six of these were at this camp because they were sent back to carry mail. Horns-in-
Front was very sick, and Cha-rá-ta had only a colt
to ride. They broke camp and marched on; the
band played all the time. Custer and Bloody Knife
came by and Bloody Knife said: "The General
says we are all marching. There are numerous enemies in the country; if we attack their camp we
are beaten, we must retreat in small groups. You
scouts must not run away, nor go back to your
homes."

The next order was that if our command was
broken up into squads or single horsemen that this
camp should be the appointed place for reassem-
bling all those that had scattered. "For my part
my heart was glad to hear the band, as far as we
could hear the band played. There were some cannon being brought along. We came to the mouth
of the Tongue River and here a camp was made.[39]

wrong. Reno (not understanding the figure of speech) said to Gerard:
"Tell him any man who is not a fool would agree with me, and that he
will show himself a soldier by agreeing with me without question."
High Bear grew very angry at this and said to Reno: "If only one of
us is to go on we will decide by a fight which one is to go. The one
killed in the fight will not go." Reno thereupon threatened to shoot
High Bear and High Bear started for him with his knife. Bloody
Knife sprang between them and said: "General Custer is my brother
and I forbid this fight." Then Bloody Knife turned to Reno and said:
"I wish for my sake you would let him go." So Reno consented to let
him go. They called Reno "The man with the dark face."

[39] This place was reached June 16th. Custer started on the morning
of the 15th. — *Report of Secretary of War*, 1876, I, p. 461.

We marched up on a hill overlooking the Elk River and then down to the mouth of the Tongue River.[40] Right at this point was an abandoned Dakota camp.[41] Here lay the body of a soldier, and all about him were clubs and sticks as though he had been beaten to death, only the bones were left. Custer stood still for some time and looked down at the remains of the soldier.''[42]

They found a burial scaffold with the uprights colored alternately black and red. This was the mark of a brave man buried there. Custer had the scaffold taken down and the negro, Isaiah, was told to take the clothing and wrappings off the body.[43] As they turned the body about they saw a wound partly healed just below the right shoulder. On the scaffold were little rawhide bags with horn spoons in them, partly made moccasins, etc. Isaiah threw

[40] Custer started on Thursday morning for the Tongue River. It was less than forty miles from the mouth of the Powder but it took about one and a quarter days to make the march. He was accompanied by six companies of the Seventh, one Gatling gun, the scouts, and pack-mules. Terry and his staff went by steamer.— Mrs. Elizabeth Custer, *Boots and Saddles*, p. 310.

[41] The Indians had occupied it the winter before. ''Miles City, Montana, was first built on the site of the camp.''— Godfrey, *Custer's Last Battle*, p. 362.

[42] On the march to the Tongue River, Custer passed through the remains of several large abandoned Indian villages. In one of these he found the remains of a soldier and his uniform, indicating that he had been a cavalry soldier. The evidence pointed toward a victim of torture and perhaps death by burning.— Mrs. Elizabeth Custer, *Boots and Saddles*, p. 311.

[43] Isaiah Dorman was a colored interpreter married to a Dakota (Sioux) woman.— Walker, *Campaigns of General Custer*, New York, 1881, p. 53.

the body into the river, and as he was fishing there later, they suppose he used this for bait. They camped here, and next day crossed the Tongue River and went through the bad lands and encamped at the mouth of the Rosebud.[44] There was a steamboat here, and the cannon were taken across the Yellowstone by the steamboat.[45] Here they waited while the scouts went up the river. Two days later the scouts returned and reported a big Dakota trail on each side of the Rosebud.[46] Opposite this camp there was another camp on the other side of the Yellowstone.[47] Six of the Crow scouts and one interpreter came across from that camp.[48] They broke camp and went up

[44] Custer reached this point June 21st.— *Report of Secretary of War, 1876*, I, p. 461.

[45] Gibbon took with him the Gatling guns which had accompanied the Seventh Cavalry to the Rosebud. They were taken across on the steamer Far West. — *Ib.*, I, p. 461, 473.

[46] Custer wrote: ''The scouting-party has returned. They saw the trail and deserted camp of a village of three hundred and eighty (380) lodges. The trail was about one week old. The scouts reported that they could have overtaken the village in one day and a half. I am now going to take up the trail where the scouting-party turned back. . . . I will move directly up the Rosebud.''— Mrs. Eliabeth Custer, *Boots and Saddles*, p. 312.

[47] This was Gibbon's command on its way up the river. In Gibbon's report of October 17, 1876, he says: ''Custer reached a point on the opposite side of the river with the whole of the Seventh Cavalry that afternoon'' (June 21st). — *Report of Secretary of War, 1876*, I, p. 473.

[48] In a letter dated June 21st, Custer writes: ''I now have some Crow scouts with me, as they are familiar with the country. They are magnificent looking men, so much handsomer and more Indian-like than any we have seen and so jolly and sportive; nothing of the gloomy, silent red-man about them. They have formally given themselves to me, after

the Rosebud River.[49] From this camp Howling Wolf, Running Wolf, and Curly Head were sent back with mail to the base camp. At this camp they issued mules for carrying supplies.[50] The scouts were given five mules to carry their supplies. Here Gerard told us he wanted us to sing our death songs. The Dakota trail had been seen and the fight would soon be on.[51] Custer had a heart like an Indian; if we ever left out one thing in our ceremonies he always suggested it to us. We got on our horses and rode around, singing the songs. Then we fell in behind Custer and marched on, and a halt was soon made.[52] Custer then ordered two groups of scouts to go ahead, one on each side of the river. Soldier led one of these bands with Red Bear, and Bob-tailed Bull the other. The scouts rode only a little ahead of the soldiers and the army camped on a flat.[53] At supper time Bloody Knife was missing, and the scouts waited for him till it was late but he

the usual talk. In their speech they said they had heard that I never abandoned a trail; that when my food gave out I ate mule. That was the kind of a man they wanted to fight under; they were willing to eat mule too.''—Mrs. Elizabeth Custer, *Boots and Saddles*, p. 312.

[49] The camp at the mouth of the Rosebud River was about midway between Tongue River and the Big Horn. — *Ib.*, p. 311.

[50] Custer said he liked campaigning with pack mules much better than with wagons. — Mrs. Elizabeth Custer, *Boots and Saddles*, p. 312.

[51] The General (Custer) told his officers at a conference on June 22d, that he intended to follow the trail until he could get the Indians even if it took him and the command to the Indian agencies on the Missouri River or in Nebraska.— Godfrey, *Custer's Last Battle*, p. 365.

[52] The command began this march June 22d at noon. — *Ib.*, *p.* 364.

[53] The command went into camp at 4 P.M., June 22d, after having marched twelve miles.— *Ib.*, p. 364.

was drunk somewhere, he got liquor from some-
body. Next morning at breakfast Bloody Knife
appeared leading a horse. He had been out all
night. Then the bugle sounded and we saddled up,
Custer ahead, the scouts following and flanking the
army that marched behind. Bob-tailed Bull was in
charge, with Strikes Two and others on one side.
About nightfall they came to an abandoned Dakota
camp where there were signs of a sun dance circle.[54]
Here there was evidence of the Dakotas having
made medicine, the sand had been arranged and
smoothed, and pictures had been drawn. The Dakota scouts in Custer's army said that this meant
the enemy knew the army was coming. In one of
the sweat lodges was a long heap or ridge of sand.
On this one Red Bear, Red Star, and Soldier saw
figures drawn indicating by hoof prints Custer's
men on one side and the Dakota on the other. Between them dead men were drawn lying with their
heads toward the Dakotas. The Arikara scouts understood this to mean that the Dakota medicine was
too strong for them and that they would be defeated by the Dakotas. Here they camped, the scouts
at the left on the right bank under Bob-tailed Bull.
They brought in two Dakota horses which had been
discovered by Strikes Two. Bob-tailed Bull

---

[54] This ''Sun-dance'' lodge was found on June 24th. The Sun-
dance was always a ceremony of great importance to the Indians. This
one had taken place about June 5th; and it was at this camp that the
Indians from the agencies had joined the ''hostiles'' in anticipation
of this event.— Godfrey, *Custer's Last Battle*, pp. 363, 366.

brought in one of them, a bald-faced bay, and Little Brave brought in the other, a black with white on the forehead (this indicated that the Dakotas had hurried away from the camp in great haste). On the right bank of the Rosebud as they marched they saw Dakota inscriptions on the sandstone of the hills at their left. One of these inscriptions showed two buffalo fighting, and various interpretations were given by the Arikara as to the meaning of these figures.[55] Young Hawk saw in one of the sweat lodges, where they had camped, opposite the entrance, three stones near the middle, all in a row and painted red. This meant in Dakota sign language that the Great Spirit had given them victory, and that if the whites did not come they would seek them. Soldier saw offerings, four sticks standing upright with a buffalo calfskin tied on with cloth and other articles of value, which was evidence of a great religious service. This was also seen by Strikes Two, Little Sioux, and Boy Chief. All the Arikara knew what this meant, namely, that the Dakotas were sure of winning. Soldier said he

[55] The Arikara scouts who were present during the giving of the narrative finally agreed upon the interpretation. The smaller buffalo charging at the larger one was Custer and his army. They would pursue the Dakotas into the broken bad-land country, represented by the shaft of stone between the two buffaloes. The Dakotas are pictured as a larger buffalo drawing back into the broken country which the Dakotas claimed as their own and would fight for to the last. The message of the picture to Custer's command was: Do not follow the Dakotas into the Big Horn country to which they have gone for they will turn and destroy you.

heard later that Sitting Bull had performed the ceremonies here in this camp.[56] After they passed this inscription of the two buffaloes charging, they came to the fork of the Rosebud River (about where the Cheyennes are now located). Six of the Crow scouts with their interpreter had been out scouting and they returned at this camp.[57] They reported many abandoned Dakota camps along the Rosebud.[58] The whole army stopped here and ate dinner on a hill. While the scouts were at dinner, Custer came to their camp with his orderly, the one who carried his flag for him. The Arikara were sitting in a half-circle, Stabbed sat at the right of Red Bear. Custer sat down with one knee on the ground and said: "What do you think of this report of the Crow scouts? They say there are large camps of the Sioux. What do you suppose will be the outcome of it all?" Stabbed jumped up and hopped about the fire, pretending to dodge the bullets of the enemy, and Custer watched him. Stabbed then said: "Chief, this is a part of our tactics; when we dodge about this way, we make it hard for the enemy to hit us. We have learned

[56] A short time previous to the battle of the Little Big Horn, Sitting Bull had "made medicine," had predicted that the soldiers would attack the Dakotas, and that they would all be killed.— Godfrey, *Custer's Last Battle*, p. 363.

[57] Captain Godfery praises the Crow scouts for their activity and for their thorough and efficient work. Half-Yellow-Face was the chief of the Crow scouts.— *Ib.*, p. 365, 366.

[58] The command passed a great many camping places on June 23d and 24th.— Godfrey, *Custer's Last Battle*, p. 366.

from the Sioux that they have shot you whites down like buffalo calves. You stand in rows, erect, and do not dodge about, so it is easy to shoot you.'' After Stabbed sat down he said to Gerard: ''I want you to tell Custer that I showed him how we fight, for when his soldiers go into the fight they stand still like targets while the Sioux are dodging about so it is hard to hit them. But they shoot the soldiers down very easily.'' Custer replied: ''I don't doubt you, Stabbed. What you say seems reasonable. I know your people; you are tricky like the coyote, you know how to hide, to creep up and take by surprise.'' The other officers came to the fire and stood around it. Custer said again through Gerard: ''My only intention in bringing these people to battle is to have them go into battle and take many horses away from the Sioux.''[59] At this Custer extended his arms and said he was glad and pleased to have with him on this expedition familiar faces. ''Some of you I see here have been with me on one or two other expeditions, and to see you again makes my heart glad.[60] And on this expedition if we are victorious, when we return home,

[59] This part of Custer's plan was very important, since, as Sheridan says in one of his reports, ''A Sioux on foot is a Sioux warrior no longer.'' This well known fact makes apparent how valuable was the work of the Indian scouts in the battle, in driving off the horses of the Dakota. General Crook in speaking of them says: ''The Sioux is a cavalry soldier from the time he has intelligence enough to ride a horse or fire a gun.''—*Report of Secretary of War, 1876,* I, pp. 447, 500.

[60] This was on the Yellowstone expedition of 1873 and the Black Hills expedition of 1874.

Bloody Knife, Bob-tailed Bull, Soldier, Strikes Two, and Stabbed will be proud to have following behind them on parade marches those who have shown themselves to be brave young men. When your chief, Son-of-the-Star, sees you on this parade, I am sure he will be proud to see his boys." To Gerard, Custer then said: "I want you to tell these young men, these boys, that if we are successful, when we return, my brother, Bloody Knife, and I will represent you at Washington and perhaps we will take you in person to Washington."

The bugles blew and they went on, Bob-tailed Bull ahead. They came upon another abandoned Dakota camp. These camps were large, one-half to one-third of a mile across. It must have rained at this camp for the sod was dug up about the tent circles to carry off the water. At this point they could see, far ahead, the hill called "Custer's Last Look," about twelve miles off. They marched towards these hills for they were to stop merely for supper and then push on all night.[61] This temporary camp was on both sides of the Rosebud and it was very dark after they had eaten supper. From across the Rosebud Crooked Horn called over: "Strikes-the-Lodge, you saddle up and Red Star also with Red Foolish Bear, Black Fox, and Bull." Forked Horn led this party and here Red Bear heard that Bob-tailed Bull was ahead and had been

---

[61] The command went into camp at sundown and the orders were to be in readiness again at 11:30 P.M. This was on the evening of the 24th.— Godfrey, *Custer's Last Battle*, p. 366.

gone since noon. This was the beginning of the
night march and they rode all night.[62] At dawn
they came to the stopping place for breakfast and
they were tired and tumbled off their horses for a
little sleep.[63] Bull-in-the-Water and Red Bear had
charge of one mule which they were unpacking and
the former said: "Let us get breakfast for if we
go to the happy hunting grounds we should go with
a full belly." In getting water for their breakfast
they had to pass through the camp of the soldiers.
The soldiers were lying in groups on the ground
snoring, for they were very tired, and lay down
where they had unsaddled. The scouts got water
and made breakfast; Bull-in-the-Water boiled
pork, opened crackers and called the rest of the
scouts. Some got up and others did not. Custer's
tent was on a little knoll at the right of the scouts'
camp. Bull-in-the-Water ate his breakfast standing up and looking around and he told the rest of
the scouts what he saw. Soon he gave a yell:
"Look what's coming," he said; "two scouts are
coming." They were Red Star and Bull.[64] Camp
broke up, the horses trotted, and the army stopped

[62] Godfrey, *Custer's Last Battle*, p. 366.

[63] The command halted a little after 2 A.M., June 25th. Some of
the men unsaddled their horses to rest them; and some coffee was made
after daylight. They rested three hours.— *Ib.*, p. 367. Also *Report of
Secretary of War, 1876*, I, p. 466.

[64] This fact is confirmed by F. F. Gerard, who accompanied the command as interpreter. These two Arikara scouts were returning from
Lieutenant Varnum, chief of the scouts, who had gone ahead to reconnoitre, and whose party discovered the camp of the Dakotas. — See
Gerard's account, Appendix, p. 132.

at a hill and Custer came down to join them. His orders were to go ahead riding hard and take the Dakota horses.[65] Stabbed rode around on horseback, back and forth, exhorting the young men to behave well and be brave. He said: ''Young men, keep up your courage, don't feel that you are children; today will be a hard battle. We have been told that there is a big Sioux camp ahead. We attack a buffalo bull and wound him, when he is this way we are afraid of him though he has no bullets to harm us with.'' He said these things for he saw many of us were young and inexperienced and he wished to prepare them for their first real fight. He was at some distance when he said this and he was rubbing some clay between his hands. Then he prayed: ''My Father, I remember this day the promises you have made to me; it is for my young men I speak to you.'' Then he called up the young men and had them hold up their shirt in front so that he could rub the good medicine on their bodies. They came up one by one, he spat on the clay and then rubbed it on their chests.[66] He had carried this clay with him for this purpose. The mule train

---

[65] Varnum and his scouts had discovered the pony herd of the Dakotas grazing in the valley of the Little Big Horn. The capture of the horses would leave them unable to move rapidly and they could not scatter and escape without them.— Godfrey, *Custer's Last Battle*, p. 376.

[66] On the forenoon of the 25th of June, the ''medicine man'' of the Arikara scouts anointed them and invoked the Great Spirit to protect them from the Sioux, Captain Godfrey says that ''they seemed to have become satisfied that we were going to find more Sioux than we could well take care of.''— *Ib.*, p. 368

with supplies was left behind and Pretty Face was detailed on the duty of looking after it.[67] The Arikara scouts who rode to the charge were: Bloody Knife, Bob-tailed Bull, Stabbed, Strikes Two, Young Hawk, Boy Chief, Little Sioux, White Eagle (he rode on a very small horse not much larger than a dog), One Feather, Black Fox, Red Foolish Bear, Goose, Red Wolf, Bull-stands-in-the Water, Charging Bull, Strikes-the-Lodge, Bull, Little Brave, Red Bear, Red Star, Soldier, and Forked Horn. Of these twenty-two men the following were killed: Bloody Knife, Bob-tailed Bull, and Little Brave. There were in Reno's camp Young Hawk, Goose, Red Foolish Bear, and Forked Horn. In the fighting line there were thirteen in all. This includes the seven already named and Strikes Two, Little Sioux, Red Bear, One Feather, Boy Chief, and Red Star. The following nine Arikara did not cross the Little Big Horn at all: Stabbed, Black Fox, Bull-stands-in-the-Water, Red Wolf, Strikes-the-Lodge, Charging Bull, White Eagle, Bull, and Soldier. The following were retained at the camp on Powder River: Tall Bear, Horns-in-Front, Scabby Wolf, Black Porcupine, Curly Head, Chará-ta, Howling Wolf, and Running Wolf. At Fort Lincoln there was the scout One Horn.

[67] General Terry in his report of June 27, 1876, says: ''Captain McDougall, with his company, B, was at first some distance in the rear with the train of pack-mules.''—*Report of Secretary of War, 1876,* I, p. 463.

Red Star's Story of His Special Scout Work ahead of the Army.

We were eating supper at the temporary camp on the Rosebud when, a little after dusk, Crooked Horn was called to Custer's quarters.[68] On coming back he said to us: "Come, Black Fox, Red Foolish Bear, Strikes-the-Lodge, Red Star (Strikes-the-Bear), and Bull." These scouts reported at Custer's headquarters and there they saw four ponies of the Crow scouts standing saddled. At his tent stood Custer with Gerard, and Gerard said to them: "Long Hair wants to tell you that tonight you shall go without sleep. You are to go on ahead, you are to try to locate the Sioux camp. You are to do your best to find this camp. Travel all night, when day comes if you have not found the Sioux camp, keep on going until noon. If your search is useless by this time you are to come back to camp.[69] These Crow Indians will be your guides for they know the country.[70] Just then Charley Reynolds (called by the Arikara, Lucky Man) came along with his horse all saddled, he was to be their interpreter. The four Crow Indians were called by the Arikara, Big Belly, Strikes Enemy, Comes Leading (Man-with-Fur-

[68] This was the evening of June 24th.— Godfrey, *Custer's Last Battle*, p. 366.

[69] When they found the Dakota's camp, two of the Arikara scouts hurried back with the news to Custer. — See Gerard's account, Appendix, p. 132.

[70] The Crow Indians joined Custer at the camp on the mouth of the Rosebud and were secured because they were familiar with the country.— Mrs. Elizabeth Custer, *Boots and Saddles*, p. 312.

Belt), Curly Head. Their interpreter was called
Man-Wearing-Calf-Skin-Vest, a white man, and he
went along, making a party of twelve. Custer said
to them: "Soon after you leave we will march on."
They started out, their horses trotted on briskly, being used to the broken country. They headed for
the Custer Butte, led by the Crows, directly from
their camp on the left side of the Rosebud. They
stopped to smoke and one of the Crows told them
by signs that by daybreak they would reach a high
mountain where they could see far, from it all the
hills would seem to go down flat.[71] They rode on and
on and reached a small grove where they smoked
again and a Crow scout told them they were near.
They came on to the foot of the mountain and the
same Crow scout, the leader, told them they had
come to the mountain and they were to climb up.
They climbed up and dismounted on the top nearest
their camp on the Rosebud and they smoked there
together on the hill. As soon as they reached the
top they unsaddled and it was just daybreak. "I
saw two of the Crow scouts climbing up on the highest peak of the hill. I had carried some coffee on
my saddle to give Bob-tailed Bull the night before.
I was told to give it to the Crow scouts, and started
towards them when I heard the Crows call like an
owl, not loud but clear (the Sioux call this way)."

71 This was the divide between the Little Big Horn and the Rosebud
known as the Little Chetish or Wolf Mountains, though the divide was in
reality only a high, broken country.— Godfrey, *Custer's Last Battle*,
p. 367.

The scouts were all sitting together when they saw the two Crow scouts coming back from the highest point of the hill. These two scouts touched the Arikara scouts and they got up to sing the song they usually sing, but the two scouts signed to them to keep silent. One of these two Crow scouts then came up to Crooked Horn and told him by signs that they had seen Dakota tepees ahead. Then all the scouts climbed up the peak to look for signs of the Dakotas. The first two Crow scouts pointed in the direction of the Dakota camp. As Crooked Horn and Red Star looked, the former said: "Look sharp, my boy, you have better eyes than I." Red Star looked and saw a dark object and above it light smoke rising up from the Dakota tepees.[72] It was at the upper end of the village, the tepees were hidden by the high ridge but the smoke was drawing out and up. Beyond the smoke he saw some black specks he thought were horses. Charley Reynolds looked a long time, then took out his field glasses and looked a long time. Then he put them down and nodded his head. He took a note book, sat down and wrote a note and got up, folded the paper, and handed it to Crooked Horn. Crooked Horn took it and turned to Red Star and said: "Boy, saddle up your pony; Bull, saddle up your pony." They had saddled up when Crooked Horn said to them: "Look, you can see the smoke of our camp."

[72] From the divide the scouts saw smoke rising above the village of the enemy. — Godfrey, *Custer's Last Battle*, p. 367.

Red Star looked and saw a cloud of smoke rising up and their way back was clear, they could follow the smoke. They started down the hill, after they were down he urged his horse on for he had the note and he paid no attention to his companion. Once in a while he looked back to see where Bull was, his horse was bad. As he came up out of hollow he saw the sentries and he gave the call, as is the custom among Arikara (the Crow scouts use the same call on bringing a message to camp), and he also began turning his horse zig-zag back and forth as a sign that he had found the enemy. When he left camp he had told Stabbed that if he came back with a message that they had found the Dakota camp, he would tie up his horse's tail, as is the custom of the Arikara. The sun was just coming up when he got to camp. The sentries began to come together in groups. Stabbed came up and said: "My Son, this is no small thing you have done." (Meaning it was a great honor, according to Arikara custom, to have brought such a message.) Red Star rode by Stabbed and got off and unsaddled. Stabbed turned and called out to the scout camp: "Why are you sleeping, Strikes-the-Bear (Red Star) has come back." Bloody Knife got up at once and met Red Star and asked him if he had seen anything. He said, yes, they had found the camp. Then he saw Gerard coming up with Custer and they came where he had unsaddled. Tom Custer was there. Custer sat down on his left knee near Red Star who was squatted down with a cup of coffee. Custer signed to Red Star asking him if he had seen the Dakotas, and he answered by a sign that he had. Then Red Star handed the note to Custer, taking it from his coat, and Custer read it at once and nodded his head. By Red Star's side was Bloody Knife and Tom Custer. Custer said to Bloody Knife by signs, referring to Tom, "Your brother, there, is frightened, his heart flutters with fear, his eyes are rolling from fright at this news of the Sioux. When we have beaten the Sioux he will then be a man." Custer then told Red Star, through the interpreter, to saddle up at once. "We are going back to where his party are on the hill," he said. Red Star was not through his breakfast, but he left his coffee, knocking it over with his foot, saddled up, and joined Custer. In the party were Custer, his bugler, Tom, Red Star, Gerard, Bloody Knife, Bob-tailed Bull, and Little Brave.[73] They rode hard toward the hill and Red Star heard a bugle as he left camp, blown by Custer's bugler, who turned backward on his horse to do so. Custer asked by signs of Red Star if the distance was short, and Red Star made signs that it was. When they got to the foot of the hill, Red Star signed that this was the place. They climbed the hill, and came to the scouts. Charley Reynolds came up and he and Custer went ahead leaving the others

---

[73] Custer went up on the divide to see for himself whether the report of the scouts was true, while the command remained concealed in a ravine where it halted at 10:30 A.M., June 25th. — Godfrey, *Custer's Last Battle*, pp. 368, 367.

behind. Charley Reynolds pointed where Custer was to look, and they looked for some time and then Gerard joined them.

Gerard called back to the scouts: "Custer thinks it is no Sioux camp." Custer thought that Charley Reynolds had merely seen the white buttes of the ridge that concealed the lone tepee. Charley Reynolds then pointed again, explaining Custer's mistake, then after another look Custer nodded that he had seen the signs of a camp. Next Charley Reynolds pulled out his field glasses and Custer looked through them at the Dakota camp and nodded his head again. Crooked Horn told Gerard to ask Custer how he would have felt if he had found two dead Dakotas at the hill. The scouts had seen six Dakota Indians after Red Star and Bull had left them. Two of them had gone over the ridge down the dry coulee and four of them had ridden into the timber at the foot of the hill. They thought the two Dakotas were planning to ambush the messengers and they wished to kill them first. They did not do so because they were afraid Custer might not like it. Custer replied that it would have been all right, he would have been pleased to have found two dead Dakotas. Then the scouts sat down and one of the Crow scouts, Big Belly, got up and asked Custer through the Crow interpreter what he thought of the Dakota camp he had seen. Custer said: "This camp has not seen our army, none of their scouts have seen us." [74] Big

74 This point whether the Dakotas knew of Custer's movements and realized he was about to attack them, is a disputed one. Captain God-

Belly replied: "You say we have not been seen. These Sioux we have seen at the foot of the hill, two going one way, and four the other, are good scouts, they have seen the smoke of our camp." Custer said, speaking angrily: "I say again we have not been seen.[75] That camp has not seen us, I am going ahead to carry out what I think. I want to wait until it is dark and then we will march, we will place our army around the Sioux camp." Big Belly replied: "That plan is bad, it should not be carried out." Custer said: "I have said what I propose to do, I want to wait until it is dark and then go ahead with my plan."

Red Star as he sat listening first thought that Custer's plan was good. The Crow scouts insisted that the Dakota scouts had already seen the army and would report its coming and that they would attack Custer's army. They wanted him to attack at once, that day, and capture the horses of the Dakotas and leave them unable to move rapidly. Cus-

frey, in his valuable account which is given the place in military history, mentions many incidents which prove that the Indians knew of the movements of the column and of an impending attack; but General Sheridan, in his report of November 25, 1876, says that he believes that "the Indians were not aware of the proximity of Custer until he arrived within about eight or nine miles of their village, and that then their scouts who carried the intelligence back to the valley were so closely followed up by Custer that he arrived on the summit of the divide overlooking the upper portion of the village almost as soon as the scouts reached it." — *Report of Secretary of War, 1876*, I, p. 444.

[75] Godfrey's account represents Custer as being well aware of the fact that his presence was discovered.— Godfrey, *Custer's Last Battle*, p. 368.

ter replied: "Yes, it shall be done as you say." The
army now came up to the foot of the hill and Custer's party rode down and joined the troop.

Narrative of Young Hawk.

The army was on the little knoll at the foot of the
hill, they were met by Custer's party from the high
butte.[76] Considerable excitement among the scouts
was to be seen. They wondered what Custer would
say when he heard that the Dakotas knew of his approach. The scouts from the hill had told them of
the six Dakotas. When the scouts saw Custer coming down they began to group themselves according
to tribes, Arikara, Crows, etc. The Arikara
grouped themselves about the older men who spoke
to the younger men as is the custom of the tribe.
Stabbed spoke to the young men[77] and Custer gave
the instructions here to the scouts through Gerard.
He said: "Boys, I want you to take the horses away
from the Sioux camp." Then Stabbed told the Arikara scouts to obey Custer's instructions and to try
and take away as many horses as possible. Custer
continued: "Make up your minds to go straight to
their camp and capture their horses. Boys, you are
going to have a hard day, you must keep up your
courage, you will get experience today." On the top
of the ridge the bugle sounded for the unfurling of

---

[76] Gerard's account confirms this statement.— See Gerard's account,
Appendix, p. 132.

[77] See Red Star's Story, p. 65.

the flag (this is what Gerard told the scouts). This caused great excitement, all made ready, girths were tightened, loads were made light.[78] Another bugle sounded and Custer ordered the scouts forward. They went down the dry coulee and when about half way to the high ridge at the right, Young Hawk saw a group of scouts at the lower end of the ridge peering over toward the lone tepee.[79] The scouts he was with slowed up as the others came toward them. Then behind them they heard a call from Gerard. He said to them: "The Chief says for you to run." At this Strikes Two gave the war-whoop and called back: "What are we doing?" and rode on. At this we all whooped and Strikes Two reached the lone tepee first and struck it with his whip.[80] Then Young Hawk came. He got off on the north side of the tepee, took a knife from his belt, pierced the tent through and ran the knife down to the ground. Inside of the lone tepee he saw a scaffold, and upon it a dead body wrapped in a buffalo robe.[81]

At the same moment he saw by him on horseback, Red Star. All of the scouts rode around to the north

[78] The troops were inspected just before the column started to the divide.— Godfrey, *Custer's Last Battle*, p. 368.

[79] Major Reno in his report of July 5, 1876, says: "We approached a deserted village in which was standing one tepee."— *Report of Secretary of War, 1876*, I, p. 477.

[80] The scouts seem to have fired this tepee for when Benteen's battalion passed it the place was burning.— Godfrey, *Custer's Last Battle*, p. 369.

[81] In his report Benteen says: "I came to a burning lodge with the dead body of an Indian in it on a scaffold."— *Report of Secretary of War, 1876*, I, p. 480.

side of the tent at full speed and turned into the dry coulee just beyond the tepee. A little further down they overtook the white soldiers and all rode on mixed together. The best mounted scouts kept up with the hard riding soldiers, others straggled behind. They crossed at the mouth of a dry coulee through a prairie dog village, turned sharp to the right, and Young Hawk saw across the Little Big Horn on the west side, Red Star, Goose, Boy Chief, and Red Bear. Young Hawk had a bunch of loose eagle feathers, he unbraided his hair and brought it forward on his head and tied it in with the eagle feathers. He expected to be killed and scalped by the Dakotas. Turning sharp to the right the battle began at about the spot where the prairie dog village stands. The first fighting began as skirmishing in front of the line.[82] Behind the ridge at the left he could see the Dakotas circling in and swarming about. The soldiers and the scouts dismounted, the horses were held in groups behind the line.[83] The soldiers formed in line toward the right, the scouts at the left out toward the ridge, while far to the left on a slant were scattered scouts.[84] Bob-tailed Bull was farthest at the left and nearest the ridge. In front of the line rode the Dakotas skirmishing back and forth. Young Hawk moved toward the right and took his position there. He saw the following scouts

---

[82] Godfrey, *Custer's Last Battle*, p. 369.

[83] Reno dismounted his command when he should have charged the village as ordered by Custer.— *Ib.*, p. 371.

[84] Reno formed the battalion with the scouts on left. — *Ib.*

in order: Red Bear, Little Brave, Forked Horn,
Red Foolish Bear, Goose, Big Belly (Crow), and
Strikes Enemy (Crow). The last scout to the left
was Bob-tailed Bull, far out beyond the others.
Young Hawk stood between Goose and Big Belly.
Behind them all, on the Little Big Horn, there appeared Bloody Knife. "He came right toward me
and I looked up and noticed his dress. He had on
the black handkerchief with blue stars on it given
him by Custer. He wore a bear's claw with a clam
shell on it." Bloody Knife spoke to Young Hawk,
calling out: "What Custer has ordered about the
Sioux horses is being done, the horses are being
taken away." Then Bloody Knife passed on back
of the line and took his stand by Little Brave. The
battle got stronger and the line curved back toward
the river.[85] Many of the soldiers were killed and
they began to fall back.[86] One Dakota charged the
soldiers very closely and was shot about sixteen feet
from the line. He rode a sorrel horse with a bald
face and his tail was tied with a piece of red cloth.
When the Dakota fell, the horse kept on coming
toward the soldiers, and Young Hawk took the horse.
He said: "I yelled to Red Bear that I wanted to give
him the horse I had captured, and for him to come
where I was." Red Bear did not come to take the
horse. A Crow Indian, Big Belly, came and said:
"My brother, I want this horse, give him to me."

[85] Godfrey, *Custer's Last Battle*, p. 371.
[86] *Ib.*, p. 271

Big Belly was Young Hawk's friend and his other name was Half-Yellow-Face. He took this Dakota horse, let his own horse go, as it was a very poor one, and jumped on the back of the Dakota horse. All this time the Dakotas had been collecting back of the ridge nearest to Bob-tailed Bull. All at once over the middle of the ridge came riding a dense swarm of Dakotas in one mass straight toward Bob-tailed Bull. At the same moment a white soldier standing nearest to Young Hawk turned to him and cried: "*John, you go!*" The Dakota attack doubled up the line from the left and pushed this line back toward the soldiers.[87] They all retreated back across the river lower down about two miles.[88] They retreated across the flat and up the bluff on a long diagonal up the steep bank, which was hard climbing.[89] The soldiers were the first to retreat across the river. Of the scouts two Crows were ahead, Half-Yellow-Face and Strikes-Enemy, then followed Red Foolish Bear and Forked Horn and then Goose and Young Hawk. When Young Hawk got back to the timber, before crossing the river, he heard Forked Horn call: "Let's get off and make a stand." He did this on account of Bob-tailed Bull who was hard pushed by the pursuing Dakotas and had fallen back nearly to the ford used by the sol-

[87] The left fell back before the dash of the Sioux.— Godfrey, *Custer's Last Battle,* p. 371.

[88] *Ib.*

[89] "It was surprising to see what steep inclines men and horses clambered up under the excitement of danger." — *Ib.*

diers. Young Hawk thought this was a general signal for the scouts and jumped off his horse and Goose followed him, also, in making the stand. They did not stop their horses, but leaped off as they were running and both shot at the Dakotas. At the crossing where the soldiers forded the river Bob-tailed Bull got over the river. The charging Dakotas turned sharply as the scouts fired at them and rode back. Young Hawk intended to fire again, but as he opened the breech of the gun he dropped his shell. The four scouts, Half-Yellow-Face, Strikes Enemy, Red Foolish Bear, and Forked Horn rode into the brush and over the river still lower down less than one-eighth of a mile. Goose and Young Hawk followed them through the brush and crossed the river where the water was deep and the brush grew very thick on the opposite bank and the horses struggled hard before getting to land. They took refuge in a thick grove of trees just across the river. The Dakotas were riding on all sides of them by this time. Here Young Hawk found the other four scouts who had ridden ahead, he did not know they were there.

All of the scouts had their horses in this grove. The Dakotas saw them ride in and began firing at them through the trees as they crouched there on horseback. He and Goose stood facing each other, then he heard a sound like a sigh and Goose groaned and called to him: "Cousin, I am wounded." Young Hawk said: "When I heard this my heart did not tremble with fear but I made up my mind I would die this day.'' Goose showed him his wound, his right hand was badly shot. Then Young Hawk took off the cartridge belt belonging to Goose and put it on himself, as he stood by the horse on the ground. He told Goose to get off his horse and he helped him dismount. Then Young Hawk was seized with rage (madness). He took off his coat and army blouse and made ready to fight for his life. Just as Goose dismounted his horse was shot down. Young Hawk put Goose against a tree and told him to hold his horse. Goose had a revolver in his belt. Just then Young Hawk saw Half-Yellow-Face crawling toward him. He said, ''My friend is being killed, he is just on the edge of the thicket.'' Young Hawk went with him crawling on hands and feet to where the Crow scout lay on his back with his hands up. The two scouts took him by his arms and dragged him back to where Goose sat with his back against a tree. He was Strikes Enemy or White Swan (Crow). He told them he was not afraid and that he was glad he was wounded. Young Hawk said: ''The sight of the wounded men gave me queer feelings, I did not want to see them mutilated, so I decided to get killed myself at the edge of the timber. Before going out I put my arms about my horse's neck, saying, 'I love you.' I then crawled out and stood up and saw all in front of me Sioux warriors kneeling ready to shoot. I fired at them and received a volley, but was not hit. I was determined

to try again and get killed, so I crawled out to the
edge of the timber in a new place, jumped up and
fired again and received a volley, but I dropped out
of sight before I was hit. Then I saw near me a tree
with driftwood piled against it, making a very good
protection and behind it I found Forked Horn lying face down to avoid being shot." When Forked
Horn saw that it was Young Hawk who had drawn
the fire of the Dakotas the second time, he scolded
him, saying: "Don't you do so again, it is no way to
act. This is not the way to fight at all, to show yourself as a mark." The Dakotas tried to burn the
scouts out but the grass was too green to burn.[90]
Young Hawk sat still for a time after being scolded
by Forked Horn and the Dakotas came closer, one
on a gray horse came very close indeed. Young
Hawk fired and missed him, then he jumped up and
shot again, killing him. The horse had on a very
handsome bridle with very beautiful trimming and
after the Dakota was shot and fell the horse kept
circling to the left, probably because he was tied by
a lariat to the body of the Dakota. Young Hawk
fired twice at the horse and at last killed him. As
the horse fell, Young Hawk gave the Arikara yell
which is always given at the death of an enemy.
Goose saw the horse fall and he called Young Hawk
to get the fine bridle for him. Young Hawk said:
"Some little time after this the Sioux came closer

---

[90] The Indians fired the grass more than once in this engagement with
the double purpose of driving the troops out and covering their own
movements.— Godfrey, *Custer's Last Battle,* p. 372.

again and I saw one Sioux coming right toward me
and I drew a fine bead on him and dropped him,
then I jumped up and gave the death call again.''
While this was going on several Dakota women rode
up and gave the woman's yell urging on the warriors to kill all the Arikara.[91] He heard them in many
places about the bushes where he lay hiding, then
they went away with the others. Some time before
noon he noticed that the Dakota attack was slack-
ening and he saw them begin to ride off down
stream, which made him think that Custer's attack
had began at the lower ford. They could see many
Dakotas crossing the river farther up and riding
down past them to the north. He said: ''After the
shooting had slackened, I stood up and looked
around. On the ridge above me on the highest
point I saw a United States flag.'' Forked Horn
then said to Young Hawk: ''My grandson, you have
shown yourself the bravest. The flag you have seen
up there shows where the pack-train is which we
were to meet and we must try now and reach it.''[92]
Custer had instructed them what to do, so as not·to
be mistaken for the Dakotas. So Young Hawk cut
a stick and tied his white handkerchief on it. They
tried to put Strikes Enemy on a horse; his leg was
pierced by a shot and his right hand also. They
were able to put him on his own horse and Goose

[91] ''The women took a hand while the battle was in progress by
stampeding the horses.''—Major James McLaughlin, *My Friend the
Indian*, p. 137, New York, 1910.

[92] McDougall with the pack-train joined Reno shortly after Benteen
did.—Godfrey, *Custer's Last Battle*, p. 373.

was mounted on the horse of Red Foolish Bear, who himself went on foot. Young Hawk rode ahead with the white flag. They rode down the stream half way the length of the ridge and as they climbed up the slope they saw the Dakotas riding back on the east side of the ridge toward the white camp. The Custer fight was over and the Dakotas completely covered the hill where the soldiers had made their last stand and were swarming toward him and beginning to fire.[93] The rest of the party turned back down the hill. Goose took Red Foolish Bear up with him and they rode back the entire length of the ridge and up at the other end into the white camp. Young Hawk remained behind and the Dakotas chased him along the ridge. He held to his white flag, waving it in front of him. The soldiers fired over him at the enemy and the Dakotas fired at him. A few rods from the camp his horse was shot down but he scrambled to his feet still carrying his white flag and ran into the camp. The first man he saw was his chief of scouts, Peaked Face (Varnum). The pack-train was there and the survivors from the fight on the Little Big Horn.[94] Then he met the officer in charge and he was glad to see Young Hawk, his face showed it. He signed to Young Hawk that the sergeant (Bob-tailed Bull) was killed and that his horse was in camp there.

[93] The Dakotas did not attack Reno for over an hour after their destruction of Custer's battalion; but now renewed the attack.—Godfrey, *Custer's Last Battle*, p. 375.

[94] They were on the bluffs across the river.— *Ib.*, p. 374

Young Hawk saw the spotted horse which belonged to Little Brave and he caught it for he had no horse of his own and he thought Little Brave must be dead. Meanwhile the Dakotas were coming up and riding around them. The other scouts who had left him now rode into the camp. Then the whole party retreated into a ravine near by (something like the ravine adjoining the house of Bears Belly, at the northwest between the graveyard and the telephone line). Here the Dakotas attacked them and the shooting made a continuous roar on both sides, soldiers and horses were killed very fast. Then the Dakotas worked around at the right and began firing into the ravine at one end. The soldiers threw up breastworks across the open end of the ravine, consisting of cracker boxes, bags of bacon, etc.[95] Young Hawk was not one of the party that built these breastworks, but he took a cracker box and put it in front of himself as he lay on the ground. The Dakotas were on every side, firing into the ravine, they came very close, crouching in lines on all sides.[96] The guns made such a noise that nothing else could be heard. The wounded men were dragged up to the breastworks as the safest place. This heavy firing went on without a break until it was dark. When it grew dark they began to take up the wounded and to place the dead at one side. They

[95] "The pack and dead animals were utilized for breastworks."— Godfrey, *Custer's Last Battle*, p. 375.

[96] The Indians had the advantage of holding the high points surrounding Reno's battalion. — *Ib.*

all stayed up until morning watching for the Dakotas and just at dawn a few shots were fired at them.[97]
Then the fight began again with heavy firing as before and this went on until late in the afternoon.[98]
All the scouts were together on the side next to
where the Dakotas came from and nearest to the
ridge. During the first afternoon an officer came
to the scouts, saying, a message was to be carried
after dark. Forked Horn said, "All right." The
officer told Goose he could not go for he was wounded and that each scout was to carry the same message. Later he came again and brought with him a
sergeant and told them that this man was to go with
them so that in case all the scouts were killed he
could tell what the conditions were in the camp.
Goose said he would go, too, although his hand was
wounded; if they were killed, he wanted all to be
killed. The officer told the scouts they were to carry
the message out to the President of the United
States, in order that all might know what had happened. They were told that they could ride government horses since they were faster than their own.
Each one was to ride hard and pay no attention to
anyone else who might be shot by the Dakotas. If
anyone fell wounded or shot he was to pull out the
paper with the message on it and leave it on the
ground so that when the soldiers came they could

[97] They intrenched themselves during the night, June 25th. Between
2 and 3 o'clock the next morning the Indians resumed the attack.—
Godfrey, *Custer's Last Battle*, p. 375.

[98] By 3 o'clock P.M. the firing had ceased altogether. — *Ib.*, p. 378.

learn what had happened and where the camp was. Then Forked Horn said that the government horses were shod and he wanted the shoes taken off so they could run better. When the messages were written for each of the scouts, the two Crow scouts stayed behind, one was wounded and the other stayed to care for him. The scouts who had the messages to carry were Goose, Forked Horn, Red-Foolish-Bear, Young Hawk, and the white sergeant. When it was dark they followed the ravine out but there the Dakotas fired on them and they all ran back.[99] The officer told them to stay until morning and start again. They stayed there all night and in the morning the Dakotas began firing again as hard as ever, the guns were going very rapidly (Young Hawk showed how the guns sounded by clapping his hands as fast as possible). Then he heard in the midst of the firing on the farther side of the ravine, the south side, not fifty yards away and very close to the soldiers, a Dakota warrior call out and give the Dakota song for a charge. The words were: "Come on, white man, come on, if you are brave, we are ready for you." As soon as he had done singing, all the Dakotas seemed to disappear suddenly and the firing stopped.[100] Then the soldiers and scouts all got up and in every direction they saw the Da-

99 Some of the scouts were sent out soon after dark, the evening of June 25th, but returned soon saying the country was full of the Dakota. — Godfrey, *Custer's Last Battle*, p. 377.

100 The Indians had nearly all left Reno at 1 o'clock. They came back an hour later and drove the men into the trenches again.—Godfrey, *Custer's Last Battle*, p. 378.

kotas retreating all on horseback toward their camp over the ridge down to the dry coulee. He saw no wounded or dead being carried off. When they climbed the ridge they could see the Dakotas in groups retreating down toward the dry coulee, all on horseback. This was now about noon. The Dakotas got to their village and the tents went down in a hurry. They thought that the Dakotas might camp where they were before. The Dakotas then moved toward the ford and reached the prairie dog village near the ford, only five tents were standing on their camping place. But the Dakotas passed the ford and went into the timber along the Little Big Horn above the ford.[101] Then smoke began to come up as from a camp. They could see the trees above which the smoke rose. As they watched, off past the old Dakota camp to the west was a ridge over two miles away and here they saw a band or body of people moving over the ridge and down toward the Dakota camp. They thought it was a band of Dakotas returning to camp from hunting.[102] Then the party approached the five Dakota tents

[101] The Indians set fire to the grass in the valley about 2 P.M. to screen their movements and about 7 P.M. they were seen going toward the Big Horn Mountains. — *Report of Secretary of War, 1876*, I, p. 478.

[102] Colonel Gibbon refers to an encounter with the scouts. ''Our scouts brought in news that they had encountered some Indians, and given chase, had run them across the Big Horn. They had dropped articles in their flight which proved them to be Crows, assigned to duty with Lieut.-Col. Custer's command. They having discovered that their pursuers belonged to their own tribe, refused to come back, and called across the river that Custer's command had been entirely destroyed by the Sioux.'' — *Report of Secretary of War, 1876*, I, p. 473.

and they rode about among them. The commanding officer said to Young Hawk and Forked Horn: "They are the white men who were coming to help us. Saddle up and go to them." So these two scouts rode to meet them down the ridge to the west and across the Custer ford until they were quite near to the party. Then they saw that they were whites and they rode back again.[103]

The soldiers in the party were busy stripping off the buckskin shirts from the bodies of the dead Dakotas there and taking their ear-rings. When the scouts got back they told the officer through the interpreter, Gerard, that the party were white men. The officer, Varnum, said that these were the white men whom they were expecting to come and help them. It was not right that Custer went ahead, he ought to have waited. The officer then said: "Now let us go and look for Custer's body."[104] Then Forked Horn, Red-Foolish-Bear, Goose, Young Hawk, and Gerard, Varnum, and some soldiers (the Dakotas called one of these soldiers Jack Drum Beater, probably a white drummer) went down to look for Custer's body. They went north along the ridge and followed Custer's trail across a

---

[103] Gibbon and Terry with their column were arriving. Two of the Crow scouts had come to camp and told of the disaster but Terry did not believe their story. He was bringing medical assistance.— Godfrey, *Custer's Last Battle,* p. 382.

[104] A detachment under Captain Benteen proceeded to the battleground. Lieutenant Bradley, Seventh Infantry, was the first of Terry's command to reach the field of carnage. — *Report of Secretary of War, 1876,* I, pp. 478, 473.

low soft place or coulee east of the hill called Custer's last stand. On the other side of the ravine they began to find dead soldiers lying with a few dead horses. When they came to the flat-topped hill where Custer fell, the officer, through Gerard, told the scouts to go off east on the hill and watch for the Dakotas lest they come back to attack them. Lying all over the hill Young Hawk saw dead horses of the Dakotas and of the whites and also many bodies of the soldiers, lying stripped. He also saw the circle breastwork made of dead horses on top of the hill.[105] Here Young Hawk took a piece of bearskin from the saddle of a buckskin horse and then shot the horse because he was very angry at the Dakotas for the death of Custer. He did not take the trappings from the horse because he could see from them that the horse was much beloved by its owner. Varnum told them through the interpreter that when they found Custer's body the bugle would call and Gerard would go and tell the scouts that they had found his body. The scouts had not been long on the hill watching (a little more than half a mile away) when they heard the bugle sound the reveille and Gerard came to tell them that Custer's body had been found. When he told them this they came back to camp, the sun was near the horizon and they were very hungry. The commanding officer said: ''Let's go to the village and follow along up the river through where the Sioux

---

[105] Godfrey, *Custer's Last Battle*, p. 375.

camped." The soldiers at the camp had been placing
the dead in rows in preparation for the burial.
They crossed lower down than where they had first
crossed, a good watering place, right below Custer's
hill (probably the Custer ford). The body of Bloody
Knife lay a little back from the brush near the ford.
He saw evidence of fighting from the Custer hill
clear to the river by the dead horses, though he saw
no bodies of soldiers. The five tepees in the deserted Dakota camp were thrown down and some of
the bodies stripped by the soldiers they had seen
there. They went on to the Dakota camp and found
the body of a dead Dakota lying on a tanned buffalo
hide. Young Hawk recognized this warrior as one
who had been a scout at Fort Lincoln, Chat-ka. He
had on a white shirt, the shoulders were painted
green, and on his forehead, painted in red, was the
sign of a secret society. In the middle of the camp
they found a drum and on one side lying on a blanket was a row of dead Dakotas with their feet toward the drum.[106] Young Hawk supposed that a
tent had covered them, with the entrance to the tent
at the side opposite where the dead bodies lay, that
is, at the holy or back side of the tent. When alive
these braves would sit on the other side and drum.
This drum was cut up and slashed. Farther on they
found three more groups of dead Dakotas lying on
canvas, buffalo hides, or blankets at the back side

---

[106] Colonel Gibbon in his report refers to the finding of the dead
warriors. — *Report of Secretary of War, 1876*, I, p. 473.

of where the tent had stood, that is, opposite the opening. All the fine buckskin shirts they had worn as well as beads and ear-rings had been stripped off by the soldiers. These groups of bodies were two, three, or four. In this camp they found evidence of great haste, bedding thrown away, bundles of dried meat dropped, etc.[107] Young Hawk picked up a paunch of pemmican and put it on his horse. Then they rode on to where the fight first began and on the west side of the river they found the mule drivers camped. On the prairie dog village at the end of the bushes they found the negro, Isaiah, lying dead; he was a Dakota interpreter enlisted at Fort Lincoln. The Dakotas had left a kettle full of his own blood close by his head and the body was very much mutilated.[108] Further on they found one of the Arikara scouts; the body was stripped, the head pounded to pieces, and a willow branch was thrust into his chest, the leafy part outside. They went on to the mule camp, and there they had supper, for it was nearly dark. While in camp Young Hawk volunteered to go with Forked Horn to the deserted Dakota camp for dried meat. They went on horseback through the dark and at the end of the camp he saw lying on the ground a long dark bundle. He cut it open and found it to be meat and he

---

[107] This is confirmed by Gibbon's report. — *Report of Secretary of War, 1876*, I, pp. 473, 474.

[108] This seems to have been the only genuine case of mutilation reported by the scouts. The bodies of the soldiers and officers were not reported as mutilated by any of the scouts. The Dakotas did not, however, spare the dead bodies of the Arikara scouts.

selected the widest pieces to take back with him. At this camp they met a white man (one of those who had come with Gibbon's command) and he had taken from the Dakota camp a stick with a scalp on it. He asked the scouts if this were a Dakota scalp and when they looked at it they recognized from the gray hair that it was the scalp of Bloody Knife, since he was the only one with hair slightly gray. The white man said the scalp was hanging from a stick standing by the body of a dead Dakota in the deserted camp. The scouts told the white man to throw it away since it was an Arikara scalp but he said: "No, if it is Bloody Knife's scalp, I will keep it for my father knew him and I will show it to him." He said he was sorry that Bloody Knife was killed and that his father would be sorry to hear it, too. He had captured twenty-five Dakota ponies which he said he would give to the Arikara scouts. His father was a well-to-do man, well known in the West, whom the Arikara called Woolly-Back, and he was at one time commandant of a post on the Yellowstone. At this post Bloody-Knife once acted as guide and hunter for him and he thought a good deal of him. Young Hawk selected for himself a black pony from the Dakota ponies the white man had captured.

In the morning they looked after the dead. Young Hawk saw one of the soldiers standing near the bank. He went close and the soldier told him to go into the river and get out the body of the dead soldier there. There were no bushes on the bank here; this was about the place where the soldiers retreated across two days earlier. He took off his clothes and went into the water nearly to his armpits. The dead soldier lay on the water, head down, and his back was out of the water; he had on trousers but no coat or shirt. It seemed to Young Hawk that the Dakotas on the other side had pulled this much of his clothes off and left him there. He and the soldier pulled the body up on the land and left it and went further up the bank. Then Young Hawk met the rest of the scouts and they agreed to go where Bob-tailed Bull was chased by the Dakotas. They found the place where he went over the bank and there they saw four leafy branches of willow sticking up in the stream. The water was shallow here and they wondered to see the willow branches there. Then they went up to a better crossing; the water was up to their hips when they crossed over. They came down on the right bank, seeing two dead soldiers stripped, all the way to the brush and there, in the edge of the brush, was the body of a sergeant (they called him "Sarge").[109] The soldiers followed and placed the bodies straight. The scouts went into

---

[109] Terry reported: Custer trail is "marked by the remains of his officers and men and the bodies of his horses, some of them dotted along the path, others heaped in ravines and upon knolls, where halts appear to have been made. There is abundant evidence that a gallant resistance was offered by the troops." — *Report of Secretary of War, 1876*, I, p. 463.

the bushes and found their coats where they had left them on the day of the fight and they put them on. They went on but found no more dead soldiers and crossed back again at a watering place for horses. As they came up the bank they found a soldier standing there and he said: "Here is one scout lying in the bushes." They could not tell who the scout was because his face and head were all pounded to pieces, but they think it was the body of Bloody Knife. Then they all got together and Gerard told them that the soldiers were going to cut poles for horse travois for carrying all the wounded. Goose said that they had better do it for him, too, for his hand was wounded. Red Foolish Bear began to fix a travois for Goose for riding jarred his wounded hand. The white soldiers collected the ten poles from the abandoned Dakota camp for the travois and the scouts wondered how they would use them. Two of the poles were lashed to the sides of two mules, one mule at each end of the poles, making mule litters. Over these poles suspended between the mules were lashed army blankets, and upon these blankets the wounded were laid.[110] A soldier walked at the head of each mule. Young Hawk took care of Goose himself, dressing his wound and bringing him food and drink. Gerard told the scouts that they were to follow the Little

[110] Lieutenant Doane, who superintended this work, received much praise for the skillful construction of the litters and the rapidity with which they were made. — *Report of Secretary of War, 1876*, I, p. 474.

Big Horn and then the Big Horn River down to
the mouth of the Yellowstone or Elk River, and
there would be a steamboat waiting for the wounded.[111] The march was very slow and wounded suffered very much.[112] Young Hawk led the pony
which dragged the travois upon which Goose lay.
At last they reached the Elk River and saw the
steamboat waiting for them near the shore with
soldiers on board. Young Hawk put Goose and his
property near the wheel, for the deck was covered.
The Crow scout, White Swan, was helped on board
by his companions. The soldiers and scouts, who
were not wounded, marched down the south side
of the Yellowstone and camped there. The next
day they saw a soldier-camp across the river.[113]
Some of the Arikara scouts had brought mail to
this camp as the boat had arrived already. Here
Goose saw Horns-in-Front, Young Hawk's father,
and told him that his son was coming down the
river. Horns-in-Front took Goose off the boat, un-
wrapped his wounded hand and washed it for him.
It was very badly swollen and Goose said he was

111 The Far West, commanded by Captain Grant Marsh, waited for
the wounded at the mouth of the Little Big Horn. — *Report of Secretary
of War, 1876*, I, p. 474.

112 General Terry in a telegram to General Sheridan dated July 2d,
reports that he commenced moving the wounded on the evening of June
28th and at 2 A.M. of the 30th they were placed on the steamer at the
mouth of the Little Big Horn. The afternoon of the 30th they reached
the depot on the Yellowstone and from there were sent by steamer to
Fort Lincoln with one of Terry's aids, Captain E. W. Smith. — *Ib.*, I,
p. 464.

113 This was the supply depot or camp on the Yellowstone. — *Ib.*

getting no attention at all on the boat. The Arikara scouts who brought the mail heard that their comrades were coming down on the other side so they crossed to the south bank and met them as they came along. Young Hawk jumped off his Dakota horse and placed the bridle in his father's hand for the horse was the gift to his father. His father was very glad to see him alive and embraced him as he used to do when he was little. The soldiers and scouts all crossed the Yellowstone to camp. The soldiers from the battlefield were in great disorder, some were hatless, others wore dirty and bloody clothing.

Supplementary Story by Soldier.

Soldier said: "I had a very poor horse and was one of those left far behind in the charge. While the other scouts are telling what they did, I sit crying in my heart because I was not in the fight. I feel that if I had owned a good horse I would have been killed because I would have been in the hard fighting."[114]

Soldier caught up with the scouts at the lone tepee but his horse was behind from the start. They started to go very fast from just beyond the lone tepee.[115] As the charge went on, the poor horses

---

[114] During the narrative by Young Hawk, Soldier went out of the house and sang a wailing song outside to relieve his feelings; no one inside paid the slightest attention although we could hardly hear what the interpreter was saying.

[115] Reno, who had orders from Custer to move forward at as rapid a

trailed out far behind. As he started on he heard
a whistle behind him and he saw Stabbed coming
up. He had been detailed to follow up a trail off
toward the left and had not gone on with the rest
of the scouts. He handed Soldier a nose-bag with
some cartridges and dried meat in it. He said: "I
give you these cartridges and if we retreat I will
come right for you and get them for I see you are
not going to keep up." At this point he heard the
firing begin, it was about two miles away. Soldier
first caught up with White Eagle and the two rode
on together until they caught up with Bull. Stabbed
rode on ahead to the end of the ridge east of the
river and the three scouts followed him. At the
ridge they began to see signs of Custer's march off
to the east. They could see the trails through the
grass. Here they found a white soldier trying to
get his horse up, he was cursing and swearing,
pounding his horse's head with his fists and kicking
him under the belly. Here the grass was much
trodden down and the trails were very plain. Soon
a little farther up the ridge, they found another
white soldier with his horse down. This soldier indicated by signs that he belonged to Custer's command. From the ridge they saw the whole Dakota
camp and the battlefield. At this point Soldier was
riding very hard. He saw Bob-tailed Bull far out at
the end of the line and many Dakotas riding behind

gait as was prudent, took a fast trot for about two miles to the ford of
the river. — *Report of Secretary of War, 1876,* I, p. 477.

the ridge at the left. He met on the ridge some of the Arikara scouts driving off the Dakota horses from between the ridge and the river. He saw some shooting at the end of the ridge over which the Dakotas were to charge later on down upon Bob-tailed Bull and the rest of the scouts. Strikes Two was one of the first he saw, and he gave him a horse. Soldier turned here and went along with Strikes Two. Then Red Star came up and said to him: "Uncle, you can have that mouse-colored horse with a spot underneath. Take that horse to ride, it is strong and you are heavy." Just at the point of the ridge where the horses came over, they met Red Wolf and Strikes-the-Lodge. Stabbed now came back and joined the party.[116] Soldier saw many Dakota tents go down and many of the Dakotas swarming back and forth at the end of the village nearest where the fighting was going on.[117] Now the Arikara scouts, Stabbed, Strikes-the-Lodge, Red Wolf, White Eagle, Soldier, Red Star, and Strikes Two, headed the horses some distance from the ridge. Boy Chief rode off with the horse Red Star had promised Soldier, till he got one. In this party also were Bull, Little Sioux, Bull-stands-in-the-Water,

[116] There was great excitement in the camp of the Dakotas.— McLaughlin, *My Friend the Indian*, pp. 169, 171.

[117] When Custer was advancing to the attack, "the chiefs gave orders for the village to move, to break up; at the time of Reno's retreat, this order was being carried out, but as soon as Reno's retreat was assured the order was countermanded, and the squaws were compelled to return with the pony herds." — Godfrey, *Custer's Last Battle*, pp. 383-384.

and One Feather. The scouts who mounted fresh horses here and rode back toward the river were: Boy Chief, Strikes Two, Soldier, Red Star, Little Sioux, One Feather, Stabbed (he did not take a fresh horse), Strikes-the-Lodge, and Bull-stands-in-the-Water (Red Bear and Strikes Two say that at this point Pretty Face came up with the mule train and that he left the train and joined the scouts).

Continuation by Red Star, Boy Chief, and
Strikes Two.

"We had no arrangement or order on the field. Strikes Two mentioned the plan first and pointed out the Sioux horses." It did not occur to them that it would make any difference what they did first as at this time there was only some light skirmishing going on. Custer's plan was for them to seize the Dakota horses across the river. They crossed the river at a point where there was no regular ford and rode after the horses of the Dakotas. There was very little fighting on the line at this time and the village was just stirring. As they headed the horses into a group, One Feather and Ptä-ä-tĕ had a bunch nearer the ford and these horses were retaken by the Dakotas who had crossed the river lower down, below the timber where Young Hawk and his party were to hide. They crossed the ridge just ahead of the Dakotas and got away with the horses. Little Sioux and Bull-in-

the-Water helped to get the horses over the ridge.
Here were all the remaining scouts who did not
cross the river. The horses were headed into a ravine east of the ridge and the scouts changed horses.
There were twenty-eight of these Dakota horses
here. As the scouts turned back to fight and rode
up on the ridge, they saw that the line was broken
and that the soldiers were coming up the hill.[118]
The Dakotas were across the river already and coming right after the soldiers. Down the river they
could see the smoke of much firing around the
grove where Young Hawk and his party were hiding. At the Dakota camp they noticed that the riders were headed down stream. Red Star saw Varnum, his orderly was with him, wounded in the
ankle. Boy Chief rode down the hill toward the
river, right among the Dakotas, to look for his
brother, Red Bear, but he was driven back.

Red Star's Additional Interview.

When Custer stood at the bank where Hodgson's
stone stands, Curly and Black Fox (Arikara) were
there with him (Goes Ahead confirms this). Pretty
Face reported that after he had joined the Arikara
scouts he saw an Arikara with a white cloth about
his head. Black Fox was the only Arikara with this
on. When Black Fox reached the mouth of the
Rosebud he met the older scouts already there, they
came out to meet him, he came on slowly. In an-

---

118 Reno's retreat from the valley.

swer to their queries he said he and Curly got together near Reno ford. Curly told Black Fox he
would take him back to show him where the soldiers
left some hard tack. So Curly took Black Fox to
the flat below the hills overlooking the present town
of Busby, north side. Curly told Black Fox that
for his part he was going home.

On the ridges overlooking the place where the
Dakotas defeated Reno, Red Star said he saw the
pack-mules unharnessed in a hollow by their drivers, and there over one ridge to the north came
three Crow scouts, Goes Ahead, Hairy Moccasin,
and Crow-who-talks-Grosventre. They came to the
Arikara scouts and told them to go back because
the army was beaten; "the Dakotas kill the soldiers
easy," that Curly, White Swan, and Big Belly
(Crow) were killed. They, the Crows, were intending to circle to the west and go home where they
lived. The older Arikara scouts told the younger
ones to take the Dakota horses down to the creek
(near the sheep ranch) and water them. While they
were watering the horses they saw the older scouts
chased by the Dakotas back on the trail and more
Dakotas coming up to the Reno ford to attack the
soldiers. Then some Dakotas attacked them and
they left the horses and escaped. The younger
scouts were Red Star, Red Bear, Bull-in-Water,
Pretty Face, Little Crow, Red Wolf, Pta-á-te (Dakota), White Eagle, Bull. The older scouts were
Stabbed, Strikes Two, Strikes-the-Lodge, Ca-roó

LINE OF MARCH OF THE TROOPS
SERVING IN THE
DEPARTMENT OF DAKOTA
IN THE CAMPAIGN AGAINST
HOSTILE SIOUX
1876
Brig Gen'l A. H. Terry Com'dg

Scale
10 5 0 10 20 30 40 50

Gen. Terry's Trail
Col. Gibbons' "
Lt Col. Custer's "

SITTING BEAR

LITTLE SIOUX   SOLDIER   YOUNG HAWK

RED STAR   BOY CHIEF   RED BEAR   YOUNG HAWK   SOLDIER   STRIKES TWO   SITTING BEAR

For explanation of the Indian sign, see p. 79, footnote 55

INDIAN SIGN LEFT BY THE DAKOTAS ON THEIR TRAIL.

The skull of a buffalo bull on one side of a pile of stones and the skull of a buffalo cow on the other side; a pole set slanting toward the skull of the buffalo cow served as a pointer or finger post. The Arikara interpreted the sign to mean that when the Dakotas were overtaken they would fight like a buffalo bull and the soldiers would run from them like women.

CURLY HEAD

Wagon

SOLDIER

STRIKES TWO

LITTLE SIOUX

YOUNG HAWK

RED STAR

RED BEAR

Boy Chief

One Feather

RUNNING WOLF

GOES AHEAD
(Crow Scout)

LITTLE BRAVE

BOB-TAILED BULL

(Dakota), Ma-tōk'-sha (Dakota), Soldier, Boy Chief, and Little Sioux.

Supplementary Story by Red Bear, beginning at the Lone Tepee. Interpreter, Alfred Bear.

Custer had ordered the charge and he also gave them orders to take the Dakota horses from their camp. The scouts charged down the dry run, and when Red Bear came to the lone tepee, the other scouts were ahead of him and were riding around the lone tepee, striking it with their whips. He did this also. All the scouts stopped at the lodge perhaps half an hour. One of them called out: "There is plenty of grub here." One Feather went into the tepee and drank the soup left for the dead Dakota warrior and ate some of the meat.[119] Just then Custer rode up with Gerard and the latter called out to them: "You were supposed to go right on into the Sioux village." While the scouts were examining the lone tepee, Custer, who was ahead of his troops, overtook them and said by words and signs: "I told you to dash on and stop for nothing. You have disobeyed me. Move to one side and let the soldiers pass you in the charge. If any man of you is not brave, I will take away his weapons and make a woman of him." One of the scouts cried out: "Tell him if he does the same to all his white soldiers who are not so brave as we are, it will take

---

[119] "This was the body of Chief Circling Bear's brother, a man of some prominence."—McLaughlin, *My Friend the Indian*, p. 130.

him a very long time indeed." The scouts all
laughed at this and said by signs that they were
hungry for the battle. They rode on ahead at this,
but Red Bear noticed that Custer turned off to the
right with his men about fifty yards beyond the
lone tepee. Gerard rode on with the scouts here.[120]
Young Hawk, Goose, Black Fox,[120a] Red Star,
Strikes Two, Bloody Knife, Little Sioux, Bob-tailed
Bull were with him, also Forked Horn, Red-Foolish-
Bear, Boy Chief, Little Brave, and One Feather.
They rode hard, charging down to the Little Big
Horn and, after crossing it, they were near the camp
of the Dakotas. When they got across, they separated again. Six of the scouts turned off to the right
sharply, where the Dakota horses were by the timber. Boy Chief and Red Star were ahead, then
followed Strikes Two, Black Fox, Little Sioux, and
One Feather. The other party led by Bloody Knife
went on toward the point of the Dakota camp.
Bloody Knife was far ahead and he brought back
three horses toward his party, calling out: "Someone take these horses back to the hill. One of them
is for me." Red Bear did not see Bloody Knife
because of the dust, but he heard afterwards who it

120 "The command moved down the creek toward the Little Big Horn
valley, Custer with five companies on the right bank, Reno with three
companies on the left bank, and Benteen farther to the left, and out of
sight." — *Report of Secretary of War, 1876*, I, p. 477.

120a Red Bear differs from the other scouts in stating that Black Fox
crossed the Little Big Horn. The others relate that he stayed on the
east of the river with the Crow scout, Curly, and the soldiers until Custer
rode with his men to attack the Dakotas at the lower ford.

was. In this party were Bloody Knife, Young Hawk, Goose, Forked Horn, Little Brave, Red Bear, Bob-tailed Bull, and the two Crow scouts. "Now we all came to the point of the Sioux camp, the guns began to go off and we got off our horses and began to shoot." The Dakotas were shooting at them from the bluffs or hills, lying down out of sight. At this time no one was riding around on horseback. They were less than a quarter of a mile off when they dismounted to fire. Forked Horn was at the point of the timber at one side and called out: "Come on this side." At the ford as they crossed down to the Dakota village, the soldiers caught up with the scouts, and the scouts crossed more at the left and Red Bear saw at his right the soldiers stringing across the river. All was excitement and confusion at this point, he recognized no white soldier or officer.[121] When Bloody Knife called out about the horses, the white soldiers had not yet dismounted. But they were all there with the scouts. The soldiers were dismounting at the time Forked Horn called and Red Bear mounted and rode to him. At the same time, he saw coming toward the line where Young Hawk stood a Dakota horse, shot in the neck or cheek. As the horse passed along, Young Hawk struck him, saying, "I strike an enemy's horse." The white soldiers were calling and shouting. As Red Bear reached Forked Horn

[121] Reno stopped here and watered the horses, delaying about ten or fifteen minutes, and reformed on the left bank of the stream.— Godfrey, *Custer's Last Battle*, p. 370.

and dismounted, Young Hawk rode up and said to him: "Uncle, I have struck the bay horse and it is mine, and I give it to you. You have a rope, get the horse for your own." Red Bear replied: "What is the use, we are fighting and I may be killed, and can have no use for it." Then Young Hawk rode back to his place. Just then he saw Little Brave riding from the timber and he said that he had heard from the yelling at the Dakota camp (he knew a little of the Dakota language) that they were about to charge. He said: "Let me fire one shot at the camp, and then let's get back to the hill, for they are too much for us." Now as Little Brave went to fire his one shot on foot, Red Bear held his horse for him. He came back at once and said to Red Bear that the Dakota were about to charge, and that they had better mount and ride back to timber and then across the river. They started to ride back and as they were going through the bushes toward the river, they received a volley from the bushes in front of them just across the Little Big Horn. The Dakotas were in ambush there, without horses. At this the scouts doubled back again to where they started from. When they rode toward the river, they saw a great mass of Dakota horsemen between the ridge and the river, riding toward the ford, yelling and firing,— it was alive with them. Red Bear dismounted when the Dakotas fired and led his horse, a leaning tree struck his saddle horn and stopped the horse. He pulled again and again at the horse's head until finally the horse came on, the saddle girth broke but he did not turn back, though he lost his extra cartridges. Then he tried to mount but twice his canteen, which he carried around his neck, got under him and he fell off. At last he mounted and rode on after Little Brave, who had not dismounted and was by this time far ahead. He soon came out of the timber where he had lost sight of Little Brave. He could see nothing on account of the smoke and dust which filled the air, but somewhere ahead he saw dimly someone riding. Just then he saw ten soldiers on horseback in full retreat toward the timber.[122] At this point there was a deep cut and the horses of the soldiers fell into it and he heard the soldiers calling out, "Whoa, whoa." He swung his horse to the left and escaped falling into the cut and he left the soldiers floundering there with their horses. He followed on after Little Brave until the dark object ahead of him turned to the left. Then he rode straight on thinking that this could not have been Little Brave and he rode past the point where he saw the rider turn to the left. His horse stumbled and fell and threw him off. The horse then ran on toward the river and Red Bear chased him. It was an open place here, a few trees and many rose bushes. A long, dry limb caught in the side of the bridle and dragged behind the horse, and stopped him so that Red Bear

---

[122] Reno's left fell back into the timber. — Godfrey, *Custer's Last Battle*, p. 370.

could catch him. The hanging rope gave him a hold but the horse was scared and jumped about a good deal. Because he could use only his left hand, he could not stop the horse very well, for he still held his gun in his right hand. Then he saw a Dakota riding toward him up stream on his right, his face was painted, the lower half red and the upper half and forehead yellow as well as the eyes. He shot the Dakota and he fell from his horse, which reared up and wheeled back. By this time he could hear nothing but the steady firing of guns and the shrill whistles of the Dakotas. He followed his horse to the river and saw him swimming about. He leaped into the water and swam to him, caught him by the mane and they went over together. As he climbed out of the water, he saw swimming behind him the horse of the Dakota he had shot. It was a dark bay and his forehead had a white streak on it, around the horse's throat was a string of deer hoofs that rattled as he swam. This horse crossed a little above him. Down stream he saw Little Brave, who had already crossed the river, and he noticed that he was wounded under his right shoulder and the blood was running down in a stream over his white shirt. Little Brave's horse was going on a slow trot toward the ridge, but not upstream toward Red Bear. He went up to where the Dakota horse had landed, intending to drive him down to Little Brave. Just then, up the bank, through the bushes at his left downstream came the horse of Bob-tailed

Bull, the reins and rope were flying, and the tail and mane floating in the wind. The horse was much frightened and ran snorting past Red Bear but a few yards away from him and Red Bear saw that the saddle was all bloody in front. Five or six white soldiers were riding through the bushes at his left, having just crossed the river. The horse of Bob-tailed Bull followed after them, and the Dakota horse he was driving dashed away after the others. (Bob-tailed Bull's saddle was an Indian saddle with a wooden frame covered with raw hide. Bloody Knife was the only one with a government saddle, horse, etc.) Little Brave was still riding on slowly and he waved his hand to Red Bear to go slowly also. The Dakotas were above them on the hills firing down at them.[128] Red Bear thought Little Brave waved his hand at him meaning that Red Bear was to catch one of the horses for him as his own was played out, so Red Bear jumped off and caught at a rope which was dragging through the bushes from one of the two horses, either that of the Dakota or of Bob-tailed Bull. But the horse was badly frightened and though he caught the rope he was dragged about through the bushes, his moccasins being lost in the river, his bare feet were torn by the rose bushes. The horse dragged him up the stream toward the end of the ridge while Little Brave and the soldiers were riding straight toward the fir-

---

[123] According to Godfrey's account the Dakotas had that advantage all the time.

ing line of the Dakotas. Finally he let go of the
rope and mounted his own horse. He did not see
Little Brave again and he thought the soldiers were
all killed. As he rode up to the end of the ridge, he
saw many soldiers retreating. Then at their head
he saw Reno, with a white handkerchief tied about
his head, his mouth and beard white with foam,
which dripped down, and his eyes were wild and
rolling.[124] The soldiers with Reno took Red Bear
for a Dakota and aimed their guns at him, but he
rode in close to Reno and struck him on the chest
with his open hand, crying "Scout, scout!" Reno
called out to him in reply: "The Sioux, the Sioux,
where?"[125] Red Bear pointed down over the ridge
where the Dakotas were. Just then an officer with
three stripes gave him some cartridges for his gun,
this officer had cartridges in boxes on his arm and
as he opened a box the cartridges tumbled out. As
the officer gave Red Bear the cartridges, he called to
him, "John, John." They then all fired at the Dakotas higher up on the ridge without taking any
aim, merely holding the guns up on a slant and firing.[126] Red Bear had a bullet cut his coat at his
arm-pit. A Dakota horse, wounded in the haunch,
ran toward them and Red Bear tried to catch him.

[124] Reno had lost his hat and had a handkerchief tied about his head,
and appeared to be very much excited."— Godfrey, *Custer's Last
Battle*, p. 372.

[125] "Reno was with the foremost in this retreat or 'charge' as he
termed it in his report."—*Ib.*, 371.

[126] In the funnel shaped ravine leading into the bluffs "the command got jammed and lost all semblance of organization." — *Ib.*

He got up in order to do so, for they were all kneeling down and firing, but the soldiers shot the horse. Here Reno made a short halt, but he could not hold his men together, they kept falling back all the time, though quite a group stayed here.[127] Then the Dakotas began to fall back and stop firing. The other remounted scouts now came up and formed a group with Reno's men. Seven scouts were missing: Young Hawk, Bloody Knife, Bob-tailed Bull, Little Brave, Forked Horn, Red-Foolish-Bear, and Goose. Red Bear had remounted when he could not catch the horse down on the flat, and the last he saw of Little Brave was his horse and the rider coming on a slow trot. Red Bear rode up to the top of the ridge and saw the Dakota scout, White Cloud, riding up from the river, and he told Red Bear that the Arikara scouts had driven off a number of Dakota horses, and they were to return but they had not yet come back. Then White Cloud said to Red Bear: "Let's go where the scouts are with the horses." White Cloud had one horse he was leading and Red Bear had picked up two where Reno had halted, and he led them. They came to a little hill and from there they saw four riders coming toward them, they thought they were Dakotas and turned to ride back to where Reno was.[127a] The riders were really Crow scouts and they seemed to recognize Red Bear, and waved to him that they were friends.

[127] Nearly all the casualties occurred during the retreat and after leaving the timber. — Godfrey, *Custer's Last Battle*, p. 372.

[127a] Red Bear is in error here. There were but three Crow scouts.

He stopped and called the Dakota scout back, for he recognized then the dress of the Crow Indian, red shoulders painted on a white shirt. The Crow scouts halted and then they rode together. The Crow scouts said that two of their number had been killed on the ridge and that they were going there and then would come back (the missing Crow scouts were those that escaped with Young Hawk). So the Crow scouts rode on to the ridge and Red Bear and White Cloud waited for them a long time. Then Red Bear said to White Cloud: "The Crow scouts will not return, let us go back to Reno." They went back and found Reno with his soldiers still there. Just then the scouts who had taken fresh horses came back. The first one to come was Bull-in-the-Water, then Strikes Two, then Red Star, Boy Chief, One Feather, Soldier, Stabbed, Strikes-the-Lodge, and Little Sioux. After awhile the other scouts came in with the herd of captured horses, about forty in number; the scouts were Charging Bull, Bull, Red Wolf, and White Eagle.[128] Where Reno was the soldiers were on higher ground, and the scouts were down the slope about ten rods off. Stabbed was riding about on horseback, making a speech. He said: "What are we doing now, we scouts? We ought to do what Custer told us to do if we were defeated. He told us to fall back to the Powder River where the rest of the scouts are and

---

[128] In Captain Godfrey's account, he mentions Crow scouts coming by driving a small herd of ponies.— Godfrey, *Custer's Last Battle*, p. 372.

the wagons and provisions.'' Pretty Face had already joined them from the pack-mule train and was there also at the time. Red Bear did not see this mule train at all. Pretty Face was probably with the herd scouts on the way back. The white soldiers were partly dismounted in their group, Red Bear did not notice any officers. The scouts were all saying among themselves that seven of them had been killed, for his part he was glad to be among them again. Stabbed told them that part of the scouts were to take the herd of horses on while the rest of them were to stay behind and keep the Dakotas off. So some of the scouts got ready to go on with the horses. They were: Bull-in-the-Water, Charging Bull, Red Wolf, White Eagle, Red Star, Pretty Face, Red Bear, One Feather, and the Dakota scout, Ptä-ä'-tĕ, and they started back with the herd of horses. Those who stayed behind were: Strikes Two, Stabbed, Soldier, Boy Chief, Strikes-the-Lodge, Little Sioux, the two Dakota scouts, White Cloud and Ca-roó, the half-breed Dakota interpreter, E-ĕsk, and Bull. The ten scouts with the herd of horses had not gone very far when another Dakota scout, Bear-Waiting (Matōksha), came in and joined the scouts, who were detailed to keep the Dakotas back. Red Bear and his other scouts rode along past the lone tepee and when they had left it six miles behind, the sun was just touching the hills. They followed the same trail they had used early in the morning. A little way out

Bull joined them; he was sent by Strikes Two with word for them to go a little faster, as he could see the Dakota tents going down, and they thought the Dakotas might chase the herd. From this point Bull went on with them and after sundown Red Wolf and Bull-in-the-Water rode ahead of the herd. It was just getting dark when they heard three shots fired somewhere ahead of the herd. The scouts behind took the alarm, swung around the herd and rode ahead, reaching the valley of the Rosebud when it was too dark to see. The two scouts who had been ahead fell back when they heard the shots and when they reached the herd they agreed that the Dakotas were coming to meet them and that they had better escape. So they picked out fresh horses and rode off ahead. When the scouts who were driving the herd from behind heard the shots ahead, they looked back on the trail and saw a cloud of dust coming, dirt flying as though from the hoofs of many horses, and they thought it must be the Dakotas coming after them. So they took fresh horses also from the herd and rode around and on until they saw the black line of timber. Here they stopped hungry and thirsty, and a big wind struck them there. They waited at the edge of the timber while one of the scouts rode on through, over a cut bank, and found a muddy water hole. He called the rest of the scouts and they led their horses over the bank; the horses slid down. Each scout then set to making his own drinking place with his hands and drinking the water as it filled into the hole. There was not enough water for any of the horses. As they talked among themselves, Whole Buffalo said that he knew the way out, so they followed him to the Rosebud, which they reached at midnight and then on to the present Cheyenne Agency, which they reached at daylight. Then they climbed a high ridge and stopped, below them was the place where the Dakotas had their sun dance (already described). The Dakota scout advised them to stay here all day until the sun went down, because they could see in every direction, back on their trail as well as in front of them. So they stayed here until sundown, some slept while others watched. Then they rode on all night until at daylight they had reached the camp where Bloody Knife had been drunk. They hunted about among the camp leavings and found meat and spoiled crackers, which they had for breakfast. They crossed the Rosebud at the point where they had crossed it on the march. Here they discovered that the scouts led by Stabbed had already crossed ahead of them in great haste. They recognized their party by the tracks of the mule ridden by Stabbed. Then they followed the Rosebud to its mouth and reached the old camp, the last parade ground. Here they found the remains of a fresh camp fire, such as cans for cooking, etc. They decided that it was the breakfast camp of the party ahead, it was now about noon. They went down the bank of the Rosebud and found some boxes of crackers partly spoiled, wet and moldy, but they made saddle packages of these and rode on. The party of Strikes Two saw them and thought they were Dakota Indians and so rode on faster out of sight. They followed the old Custer trail very slowly until they were near the Tongue River and then camped on top of the ridge in the timber. In the morning they reached and crossed the Tongue River and found the place where the soldier had been clubbed to death. On the top of a range they went on and reached the Powder River camp. Here they found the party led by Strikes Two and a company of infantry, with a wagon train. The commander was called Wearer-of-the-White-Hat, he was from Fort Buford. This officer had two interpreters, a half-breed Dakota called The Santee, and a Grosventre called Crow-Bear. They told the officer through these interpreters all that they knew about the fight. The officer called the scouts all together and told them to bring in their horses. He picked out two of the best horses for the scouts who were to carry word to the officer who had gone up the Elk River on a steamboat to the mouth of the Big Horn River.[129] He selected Foolish Bear and White Cloud to carry the orders. These two scouts swam their horses over the Yellowstone or Elk River, swimming themselves and pulling a small raft behind them, which had

---

[129] This was General Terry who went up the Yellowstone on the Far West. — *Report of Secretary of War, 1876,* I, p. 463.

upon it their guns and a small bag with the message in it. These scouts rode to the mouth of the Big Horn and after a time (several days), they came back and called for Strikes Two and Bull-in-the-Water to cross over to them and carry the mail to Fort Buford. Foolish Bear and White Cloud then recrossed the river and joined the other scouts.

Later Supplementary Story by Running Wolf.
Interpreter, Alfred Bear.

Running Wolf enlisted in the spring of 1876 at Fort Lincoln with six others, Young Hawk, Horns-in-Front, Tall Bear, Foolish Bear, Red Foolish Bear, and Charging Bull. They started from Fort Berthold and camped over night at Fort Stevenson. Big John, an Arikara scout, was in charge of the party. The same man (already referred to) was in charge at Fort Stevenson. They camped next day just north of where Washburn is now and reached Bismarck by noon and went across the river in a steamboat. Next morning Gerard took them to headquarters where they were enlisted. The camp of the scouts was at the foot of the hill, but the next day they joined the soldiers in camp farther back from the river. While in camp they learned that Custer was at Washington and they were told that on his return he would start on the expedition.[130] After Custer returned, six days went by

---

[130] "Lieut. Col. Custer of the 7th Cavalry was at first assigned to the command of this force; but under subsequent instructions I assumed

before the expedition started. On the last day, Bob-tailed Bull and Soldier were called to headquarters and the former was made sergeant. Then Gerard notified them next day to get ready for the parade, for they were to march Indian style, singing their own songs. This was to be the beginning of the first day of the march, and the songs they sang at that time were some of the same ones that were given when this story was told at the council at Bear's Belly.[131] After the parade, the scouts led the march with Custer ahead, and the white cavalry bringing up the rear.[132] The scout chief was Varnum (Peaked Face), he camped all the way near the scouts and had one orderly and a cook, who served his meals in his own tent. The army camped at noon and remained there till next morning. When they stopped

the command in person, Lieut. Col. Custer being assigned to the command of his regiment." — *Report of Secretary of War, 1876*, I, p. 459, (Terry's report).

[131] "The Indian scouts themselves beat their drums and kept up their peculiar monotonous tune, which is wierd and melancholy beyond description. Their war-song is misnamed when called music. It is more of a lament or a dirge than an inspiration to activity. This intonation they kept up for miles along the road."— Mrs. Elizabeth Custer, *Boots and Saddles*, p. 262.

[132] "The cavalry and infantry in the order named, the scouts, pack-mules, and artillery, and behind all the long line of white-covered wagons, made a column altogether some two miles in length." Mrs. Custer rode with her husband at the head of the column during the first day's march, returning to the post from the first camp beyond the fort. The arrangement with regard to the scouts, referred to above, undoubtedly lasted only the first day, while Mrs. Custer rode with the General, after which they would ride at the head of the column with the commander.— *Ib.*, p. 263.

for dinner the next day it started to rain and they
went no farther that day. The next morning they
went on and made a second camp west and north of
the Heart River on a big flat. The next day there
was no stop for dinner and the scouts called Camp
No. 3, Turkey Buzzard Camp. From this camp at
sunset the mail was sent back by two scouts, One
Horn and Red Foolish Bear. The soldiers were
paid off at the first camp. A herd of cattle was
driven along with the army. The army ate dinner
at Big Mountain (Butte) and made Camp No. 4 in
a wide valley. They ate dinner the next day on
the open prairie and Camp No. 5 was made at what
is now Hebron. At the dinner stop next day it
rained and the army camped there close to Young
Man's Butte, Camp No. 6. Dinner was eaten the
next day on a muddy flat and because the roads were
too heavy for the loads, the army camped here, Camp
No. 7, beyond Young Man's Butte. The army took
dinner next day at a coulee east of the present station of Dickinson. At Camp No. 8, in the middle of
the night, Red Foolish Bear came in and reported
to Bob-tailed Bull that he had left Red Bear back
on the trail with a played-out horse. Bob-tailed
Bull took a party back on the trail for Red Bear
and brought him to camp early in the morning.
Strikes Two gave Red Bear his spare horse. The
dinner stop that day was in a coulee with trees, and,
because it was muddy, the army camped here, Camp
No. 9. The army reached the Bad Lands by noon

the next day and camped here, Camp No. 10.[133]
Custer went ahead to look for a trail for the wagons.
The next day the army went into the Bad Lands and
Camp No. 11 was just inside. Timber was cut and
carried along for bridges. The orders next morning were that each man was to carry his own dinner.
Camp No. 12 was made at the Little Missouri Valley, near Soldier Butte.[134] The next day they passed
the Butte and camped just beyond, Camp No. 13.
It snowed here in the night, the snow was from two
to three feet on the level. The army stayed here all
day and the next night, and by the following day
the snow had melted a good deal. So they went on
through the mud and slush, which was heavy for
the teams, along a flat-topped ridge. At the end of
the ridge about noon they met Crow Bear, a Grosventre scout on horseback. He had come from Powder River with the mail and after dinner he turned
back again. There was no stop for dinner that day.
The army marched down a coulee to Beaver Creek
and made Camp No. 14. The next day they followed
up Beaver Creek to the end and made Camp No. 15.
The next day the march was made on the open prairie, a flat land, and in the distance they could see
blue hills. Camp No. 16 was made on the open prairie. They marched on next day toward the blue
hills, toward a coulee with cottonwoods, Camp No.

---

[133] The Bad Lands of the Little Missouri were reached on May 27th.
—Godfrey, *Custer's Last Battle*, p. 361.

[134] "On the 31st we crossed the Little Missouri without difficulty."
— *Ib.*

17.[135]   The Dakota scouts said that their name for
the place was Cottonwood Creek. They reached the
foot hills by dinner time and after dinner they went
on until they reached the point where the Powder
River enters the Bad Lands. Here they made Camp
No. 18. In the morning Custer came to Varnum's
tent and called for Bob-tailed Bull. He told Bob-
tailed Bull that he wanted seven scouts to be sent
ahead to look for signs of the Dakota, four Dakota
scouts and three Arikara. The Arikara scouts sent
out were Young Hawk, Forked Horn, One Feather.
The Dakota scouts were Ca-roó, Ma-tōk'-sha, Buffalo Body (Pta-á-ate), and White Cloud. Some
white soldiers went along, too, and they marched in
two lines. The orders were not to return until they
had found fresh signs of the Dakotas. They were
to report at the base camp at the mouth of the
Powder River. Camp No. 19 was made at the mouth
of the Powder River and there was a steamboat here.
Two sick scouts, Horns-in-Front and Cha-rá-ta
(Wolf), were left here at this camp, in care of Tall
Bear. There was a store tent here in charge of a
white man and he sold the hindquarters of a deer
to the soldiers at $4 each. The wagons were left
here with a guard of soldiers. The army marched
on to Tongue River and camped up from the mouth
about two and one-half miles, Camp No. 20.[136]   At

---

135 There is a slight discrepancy between the stories of Red Star and
Running Wolf with regard to Camps 17 and 19.

136 Custer reached the Tongue River on the 16th of June.— *Report
of Secretary of War, 1876,* I, p. 461.

this point the scouts sent back a report to Custer as to what they had found. They crossed the Tongue River and went on to a plateau, Camp No. 21. The next day they camped on a flat-topped elevation, quite a distance from the Rosebud and one mile from the Elk River, Camp No. 22. Camp No. 23 was on the high ground about a quarter of a mile above the mouth of the Rosebud River. Camp No. 24 was on the flat at the mouth of the Rosebud.[137] The next morning Custer and his brother Tom came to the scout camp to see Soldier, Bob-tailed Bull, and Bloody Knife; Gerard was interpreter. While they were there at the camp, Young Hawk told them that on this river they had found a fresh trail and camp of the Dakotas. At this time the steamboat was there landing boxes of hardtack crackers and they were opening the boxes. Just then the bugle blew and they all saddled up and rode to where the crackers were and each one took rations enough to fill his leather saddle bags. Custer was then writing dispatches and six scouts were detailed to take them to the base camp at the mouth of the Powder River. The scouts were: Foolish-Angry Bear (in charge), Running Wolf, Howling Wolf, Curly Head, Goose, and Young Hawk. But afterward, when Custer found out what scouts were in the party, he detained Young Hawk and Goose, because they had found traces of the Dakotas and he knew that Young Hawk could shoot well and would kill

[137] This camp was made on June 21st. — *Report of Secretary of War, 1876*, I, p. 461.

some of the enemies. He remembered Young Hawk
from his Black Hills expedition and also Goose.[138]
The dispatches were ready and the four scouts who
carried them received Custer's orders to stay at the
base camp after delivering the dispatches. This was
3 or 4 o'clock in the afternoon. The scouts detailed
for this duty were not anxious to return to the
base camp, they preferred going on with the rest.
They traveled all night, ate breakfast, traveled all
day and all the next night until, at sunrise, they saw
the wagons at the base camp one and a half miles
away. Two Arikara scouts rode out of the camp to
meet them, Charging-up-the-Hill and Wagon, these
two had been left behind at Fort Lincoln. They all
talked together for some time and then they went
down to the base camp. It was then about noon and
the six scouts were at once detailed to carry some
Fort Lincoln dispatches on to Custer, and along
with them went a white soldier. Running Wolf led
this party of scouts and there were also Howling
Wolf, Horns-in-Front, Tall Bear, Charging-up-the-
Hill, and Curly Head. After dinner they started
back and rode until the middle of the night, when
they were too tired to go further and camped in order to sleep. In the morning they traveled on and
reached a place to camp at dark near the Rosebud.
The next morning they came up to the mouth of the

---

138 It was Goose who told Custer about the wonderful cave in the
Hills, before the expedition of 1874 started.— Mrs. Elizabeth Custer,
Boots and Saddles, p. 299.

Rosebud where the crackers were landed, and in the distance they saw men there. They thought it was the Dakotas and turned sharp into the timber on the Rosebud. They stayed here all day until sunset and then Tall Bear said, "Let's go back to the base camp." But the soldier, by signs and the use of a few Dakota words, told them they could not go back, that they must carry the dispatches on to Custer. He proposed to them that they cross the Rosebud after dark and swing around the Indians, whom they supposed were the Dakotas, and so go on to Custer. They followed his directions, they forded the Rosebud, the water was up to their arm-pits. They traveled all night, and the next day about 4 o'clock they saw the camp of soldiers at the mouth of the Big Horn.[139] They thought this was Custer's trail they were following because it was too dark to see where he had gone and then, too, they feared the Dakotas, whom they supposed were seen at the mouth of the Rosebud. Those whom they had seen there were really the party of Strikes Two, retreating to the base camp from the fight on the Little Big Horn. This party of scouts had ridden ahead of those detailed to carry off the horses, they had passed them in the night in their hurry to keep out of the way of the Dakotas. At the Big Horn camp the scouts learned all the news of the Custer fight.

---

[139] Terry was in command of this camp on the Yellowstone near the Big Horn River. It was a supply depot.— *Report of Secretary of War, 1876,* I, p. 464.

Terry was in command here, he was called by the Arikara, Man-Wearing-the-Bear-Robe. Terry once wore a coat made of bearskin and the older scouts remembered him for this. Running Wolf does not know who told the news of the fight but all the scouts learned of it. The steamboat had gone up the Big Horn a little way, as far as the depth of the water would allow.[140] It was understood that this boat had gone up for the wounded and survivors of the Custer fight. It was about noon when they learned this news. Then two scouts came in from the base camp, Crow Bear and a white soldier, bringing news of the arrival of Strikes Two and his party, with their news of defeat and loss. It was reported: "All of the white soldiers and some of the scouts were killed." Then Crow Bear said: "The scouts killed are Bloody Knife, Bob-tailed Bull, Little Brave, Forked Horn, Red-Foolish Bear, Young Hawk, and Goose," for these scouts were not in the two parties escaping to the base camp. Crow Bear and the white soldier were sent back immediately to the base camp with dispatches. Then Terry came to the scout camp and gave Running Wolf a pair of field glasses and told him to go up the Big Horn to the hills and look out for the returning steamboat. Running Wolf took Charging-

---

140 Terry reports: "Thanks to the zeal and energy displayed by Capt. Grant Marsh, the master of the steamer (Far West), the mouth of the Little Big Horn was reached by her, and she was of inestimable service in bringing down our wounded. They were sent upon her to Fort Lincoln." — *Report of Secretary of War, 1876,* I, p. 465.

up-the-Hill and rode off on this duty. At night they
came back and reported they could see no boat. The
next morning Terry again came to the camp and
gave Running Wolf the same directions, handing
him his own field glasses. Terry told Howling Wolf
to go along also, to see if the steamboat was coming.
They returned for dinner and Running Wolf handed back the glasses to Terry. Then about 3 or 4
P. M. he heard a sharp whistle upstream and knew
that the steamboat was coming to them. They went
down to the bank, scouts and all, and they saw a
white canvas cover over the whole deck and wounded soldiers lying under it in the shade. On the prow
of the boat they saw Strikes-Enemy, the Crow scout
who was wounded. The soldiers began taking off
the wounded and putting them down on the canvas
lying on the bank.[141] When this was about half
done Running Wolf noticed Goose near the engine
room with a blanket over his shoulders and his hand
wounded and wrapped up in his chest. Then he
went to him with another scout and helped him up
the bank. Goose said to him: "We have fought the
fight with the Sioux, we were cut off in the timber
with the Sioux on every side but we escaped alive.
The other scouts are coming on after the boat on
foot." Soon they saw the white survivors coming
along, and the four scouts last of all, Young Hawk,
Red-Foolish-Bear, Forked Horn, and a Crow scout,

141 The wounded were brought to the depot on the Yellowstone on
the afternoon of June 30th. — *Report of Secretary of War, 1876*, I, 464.

Half-Yellow-Face. As he came up Young Hawk began to tell the story of the fight. "Bloody Knife is dead," he said, "Bob-tailed Bull is dead and Little Brave is dead. We could not find the body of Little Brave but the bodies of the others we found with their heads pounded and smashed to pieces." Young Hawk was leading the spotted pinto that had belonged to Little Brave. Young Hawk then related his story of his fight in the timber and also what took place after he reached the camp in the ravine. The next morning they put the wounded soldiers back into the boat with the scout, Goose, and they went down the river in the boat.[142] Terry and the Chief-with-a-Red-Nose were in command.[143] They told all the scouts to follow down the east bank of the Yellowstone (Elk) and look for a Dakota crossing over to the western side. The scouts were gone ten days and in the party were: Forked Horn, Horns-in-Front, Red Foolish Bear, Charging-up-the-Hill, Tall Bear, Young Hawk, Running Wolf, and Wagon. Two of the scouts stayed behind in Terry's camp, Curly Head and Howling Wolf. They hunted for the Dakota trail across the river for ten days. They returned to

[142] The steamer bearing the wounded reached Fort Lincoln July 5th, and brought the first news of the disaster to the post. — Mrs. Elizabeth Custer, *Boots and Saddles*, p. 268.

[143] The Chief-with-a-Red-Nose appears to be Colonel Gibbon, who joined Terry with his command July 2d, and remained in the Yellowstone camp until July 27th, when it was transferred to the new depot at the mouth of the Rosebud. — *Report of Secretary of War*, I, pp. 465, 474.

Terry's camp and Soldier was not there. The camp
was changed to the mouth of the Rosebud and so
was the base camp at Powder River, making one
base camp.[144] The two commanders said they must
go up the Rosebud and search for Sitting Bull.[145]
Half way up the Rosebud they met Crook in charge
of a body of foot and some mounted scouts, Arap-
pahoe or Shoshone. Here all the scouts got together,
Terry and the Chief-with-a-Red-Nose, with Varnum and Crook and their men.[146] They followed
the Dakota trail to the Tongue River where they
camped. Next day they went on to the Powder
River where there was big timber on the bank. Here
they camped. The next morning the surviving soldiers of Custer's command, all the Arikara scouts,
and Crook's Indian scouts marched under Terry
and Varnum down to the mouth of Powder River
and camped there.[147] Crook's command and all the
rest of the soldiers stayed here. At the mouth of
the Powder River the Crow scouts and Crook's

[144] "The depot was moved to the north bank of the Yellowstone, opposite the mouth of the Rosebud and the troops from both above and
below were brought to it." — *Report of Secretary of War, 1876*, I, p.
465.

[145] "On the third, the crossing of the river commenced. It was completed on the 7th, and on the 8th of August the march up the Rosebud
began." — *Ib.*

[146] On the 10th of August, Terry and Gibbon met Crook and his command coming down the Rosebud and the united commands resumed the
march on the Indian trail which Crook was following. — *Ib.*, p. 475.

[147] "The command moved across to the Tongue River, down that and
across to the Powder River, and down that to its mouth, which it reached
on the 17th." — *Ib.*

scouts went back to their reservations. The rest of the camp returned to Crook's camp on the Rosebud but Crook had already gone on the Dakota trail. The Chief-with-a-Red-Nose and some other officers came to the camp of the scouts with a letter in his hand. He selected a detail of seven scouts to carry the letter to Crook while the rest of the camp were to go back to the base camp. The seven scouts were Soldier, Black Fox, Charging-up-the-Hill, Boy Chief, Young Hawk, Running Wolf, and Ca-roó (Dakota). They carried the letter to Crook's camp and delivered it to him. They found out that he was on Sitting Bull's trail. Crook notified them they were to stay and scout for him, reporting every other day, so they followed these orders day by day under Crook's command. When they came to Beaver Creek, Running Wolf and Young Hawk were out hunting by themselves on a ridge and the rest of the scouts were together.[148] When Running Wolf and Young Hawk got to Beaver Creek, they found the rest of the scouts there and also a party of Indians on foot. There were cavalry here also under a separate commander. Ca-roó had already been sent back to Powder River with the mail but he soon returned and reported that the orders from Beaver Creek were that he was not to go with the mail but in place there were to go Soldier, Boy

---

[148] Crook's column moved south on the Indian trail to a point on Beaver Creek, opposite Sentinel Buttes, where the trail split into several smaller ones. — *Report of Secretary of War, 1876*, I, p. 509.

Chief, Black Fox, and Charging-up-the-Hill. The
sun was just setting and the three scouts camped,
that was all there was left of the original scouting
party. The rations they got were two crackers
apiece and two spoonfuls each of coffee and sugar.
Just as they were going to bed somewhere about
midnight they heard the sound of horses coming up.
They were the Dakotas coming on horseback and
soon they began firing at the camp. The soldiers
began to run out of tents, half asleep, sometimes
without guns or anything to fight with. The orders
were that they were to make for a ridge of higher
ground. The Dakotas were circling and firing into
the camp and the soldiers were firing back, making
it quite light. The cavalry did not at first take part
in the fight but presently the bugle sounded, they
got lanterns and saddled up and began to take part
in the fight, too, and the Dakotas retired into the
darkness. The scouts were on a little hill and did
not take much part in the fight. The next day the
soldiers stopped following the Dakota trail and
came to Soldier Butte, where they camped. They
reached the Little Missouri and found an old Dakota camp there and camped for the night. About
noon they found a Dakota camp in the timber but
the officer would not let them fight the Dakotas, for
he said he wanted them to stay by the camp and
that he would camp on Custer's old camp site east
of the Rosebud Butte. They reached this spot about
5 P.M. About dark the scouts noticed a confused

gathering of men in the cavalry camp and it looked strange to them. Ca-roó went up to see what was going on among the soldiers and Young Hawk followed him and then, calling Runing Wolf by name, he said: "These men are writing letters to go back to Fort Lincoln and we are to carry them tonight." They had supper and at sunset they started out with the letters for Fort Lincoln. They rode all night and then stopped to eat and feed their horses at Young Man's Butte. They rode all day and reached Sentinel Butte when it was very dark. They traveled all that night and all the next day, reaching Fort Lincoln when it was nearly dark. Running Wolf was discharged in January, 1877.

Later Supplementary Story of Little Sioux.
Interpreter, Reuben Duckett.

It was early in the morning, just at sunrise, and there came down from the butte, Red Star and Bull. By this time the army was all together and the mule pack train was with them. Custer told all the scouts to come to him and they made a circle about him.[149] He said to them: "Well, I want to tell you this, the way I want it. We all want to charge together and after we get to the Sioux camp I want you to run off all the horses you can." Then the charge began for the Dakota camp; they went three or four

---

[149] At the same conference the Indian scouts told Custer that he would find enough Dakotas to keep him fighting two or three days. The General smiled and remarked, "I guess we will get through with them in one day." — Godfrey, *Custer's Last Battle,* p. 367.

miles and then Custer went up on the high butte
and came down again after seeing the Dakota camp.
The scouts led on with the charge and reached the
lone tepee about noon. It was about as far to the
Little Big Horn as it was from the high butte to
the lone tepee.   It was nearly 3 o'clock when they
reached the Dakota camp.[150] They rode at full speed
with Custer and Little Sioux about the middle.
When he reached the river he saw going up the bank
on the other side, Young Hawk, Strikes Two, Boy
Chief, and Goose. As he came up the bank he saw
before him a curved, flat space covered with sage
brush and with timber at the right. The soldiers
were forming a line at right angle to the timber
and then the firing began. In front of the soldiers,
while he was a little way from the bank, Little
Sioux saw Black Fox[150a] and Forked Horn. Away
to the left and in front of the soldiers, near some
buttes, he saw Bob-tailed Bull. Some Dakotas were
riding in between Bob-tailed Bull and the soldiers.
Little Sioux was about half way to the line of soldiers with others all around him, and then he saw
Bloody Knife swing in from the timber along which,
from the direction of the Dakota camp, he was driving three horses. Bloody Knife was his uncle and he
came up to him and said: "Take these horses away
back, this is what Custer told us to do." Little

---

150 Little Sioux places the time too late. Captain Godfrey says it
was 2:30 P.M. when Reno was joined by Godfrey and then Custer's battalion was being surrounded and wiped out. — Godfrey, *Custer's Last
Battle*, p. 374.

150a For Black Fox being here see *auto.*, p. 122, footnote 120a.

Sioux paid no attention and Bloody Knife turned back without waiting to see what became of the horses. With Little Sioux there were Red Star, Strikes Two, and Boy Chief. As they stood there together looking across the river they saw at the foot of the ridge (about where they were to cross later) three women and two children coming across the flat running and hurrying along as best they could, on a slant toward the river. Little Sioux fired twice at them and so did Red Star. Then all four of the scouts rode through the timber toward the river to kill them. But just at this point they saw across the river on the flat a large herd of about two hundred Dakota horses in the sage brush, so they stopped pursuing the women and children and started after the horses.[151] Little Sioux had no trouble at either bank, he rode his horse swimming. On the opposite side there was much sage brush and willows and the four all crossed together. They started to head the horses upstream. Red Star rode farthest to the left, then Boy Chief, then Strikes Two, and last of all Little Sioux. While they were driving the horses he first saw the tepees of the Dakotas, three-quarters of a mile away across the river, just the tops of the poles and very many of them.[152] They had ridden farther ahead than the battle line of the soldiers, that is, farther down-

---

151 The Dakotas had an immense pony herd. — Godfrey, *Custer's Last Battle*, p. 367.

152 The village was very large. — *Report of Secretary of War, 1876,* I, p. 463.

stream in order to head off and drive the horses back to where they could get them away from the Dakotas. They had hardly headed the horses before the Dakotas came across the river from the village where he had seen the tops of the tepees and from there they carried on a running fight up the valley for over a mile with the pursuing Dakotas chasing and firing at them. They reached and crossed the high bluff, at which point was the hardest fighting, and the Dakotas chased them back on the trail seven or eight miles. This fight for the horses was kept up until nearly dark or until the red blaze from the guns could be seen and there were only five Dakotas left. These seemed to have ridden around in front of the herd and attacked the scouts as they went by. The flat between the ridge and the river was about three-quarters of a mile wide and they drove the horses nearer the river than the ridge. They crossed the ridge because it curved in front of them and they did not turn out of their course. Where they crossed the ridge, was a mile below the first crossing and about three-quarters of a mile from the second crossing. The two places on the river where Little Sioux crossed were about a mile apart. While he was driving off the horses on the flat he heard the battle going on very plainly at his right and on his left also. Slightly behind him he heard sounds of another battle but not quite so plain. As Little Sioux came up the ridge he met the other scouts that had been left behind and they all went on together. From the ridge he saw that the battle was over, dead men and horses lay all the way from where the battle line was to the river, and also on the bank and up to the hill. They rode on and looking back they saw some dismounted soldiers, who had straggled up from the river, fighting the Dakotas back. He saw a dead soldier lying just where he came up over the ridge on the hill. Here Little Sioux's horse played out, the one he had ridden from the first. He was riding ahead of the other scouts when he saw a black horse with a piece of buckskin around his neck from which hung a bell. He threw himself off his horse, caught the Dakota horse, put his own saddle on it, and turned his own horse loose, all of this during his ride up the hill. At the time he looked back to the battle-ground he also looked toward where he had heard the firing at his left. There he saw, about two miles west, near enough to hear the guns, along the ridge, a high sloping hill, the sides of which were covered with Dakota horsemen, thick as ants, riding all about. At the top some soldiers were lying down and were shooting down at the Dakotas, who were firing back. He noticed many little fires on the prairie where the first fighting took place, much smoke but no blaze. He saw also on the hill at the south, groups of Indians moving off here and there. He noticed that these groups scattered as they got up higher and broke up in every direction, this was about three miles off. He saw also on the battleground Dakotas riding about among the dead bodies shooting at them.[153] There were five Dakotas in the last attack which was made on the scouts who were driving off the herd of Dakota horses. Stabbed told some of them to dismount and hold back the enemy. Those who stopped to do this were Little Sioux, Soldier, Strikes Two, Boy Chief, Stabbed, and Strikes-the-Lodge. When the four scouts met the others at the top of the hill some of them stayed behind to fight back the Dakotas. These were: Soldier, Little Sioux, Stabbed, Strikes-the-Lodge, Strikes Two, and Boy Chief. They fought on foot to hold back the Dakotas who had by this time killed all the dismounted soldiers. Their horses were tied to their cartridge belts by a loose slipknot and when riding this rope hung in a coil on the saddle-horn. This device was used by all the Indians so that they might never be in danger of losing their horses in battle. When this group of scouts had stopped the Dakotas and driven them back, it was about an hour from sunset and they tried to find the herd but missed the way for a time. In the last fight with the five Dakotas, already referred to, the herd of horses was so close that the firing scared them and in spite of all the other scouts could do the whole herd was lost. Little Sioux fell back now with the other five scouts for they thought all the soldiers were killed and all the horses lost. Stabbed drove his horse

---

[153] Captain Godfrey confirms this statement. — Godfrey, *Custer's Last Battle,* p. 373.

and rode a mule taken from the big herd when the scouts first met him. They rode all night long and all the next day till evening without stopping and they came to where the steamboat unloaded. Here were some spoiled crackers and they made camp all night and rested and ate. While they were in camp here they were seen by the party led by Running Wolf, who thought that they were Dakotas. After sunrise the next day Black Fox came up and joined them. After he was seen in distance Little Sioux was sent back to meet him and he called to him that he was an Arikara, but Black Fox could not hear him for the wind blew toward him and he thought it was a party of Dakotas. Black Fox got off of the Dakota horse he was riding, leaving the saddle, and mounted his own, bareback. He rode into a blind washout with high banks but here he heard Little Sioux's voice echoing back from the high bank and he recognized him and rode out again. He was glad to see Little Sioux and gave him the horse he had caught. The six scouts slept under the roots of a fallen tree and they had a fire. They were cooking some camp leavings when Black Fox came in sight a long way off, about 8 o'clock. The seven scouts traveled all day and camped at the mouth of Tongue River and slept there. The next day they came to the Powder River base camp just as the bugles were blowing for dinner. Some soldiers came out to meet them and they told them what had happened but the soldiers did not believe them. Then the commanding officer called them in and the scouts told him what they knew. He said nothing when they had finished and sent them out again. In camp they found four scouts, Horns-in-Front, Cha-rá-ta, and two others. About three days later the commanding officer ordered them to bring their horses up for inspection, as mail was to be carried. But the horses were all worn out so two mules were used instead. He sent the mail out by two scouts, Crow Bear and a half breed, to General Terry on the Big Horn River. No other scouts had come in yet. Before they had reached Terry's camp the steamboat came in with the wounded. Until the boat came in seven scouts were missing, the three who were killed and the three with Young Hawk, besides the interpreter, Gerard. The steamboat took the scouts across the river, about twenty-four of them, and they went up the river and met the Crow Indians who had come together too late to help Custer at the mouth of the Rosebud. They recrossed the Elk River by steamboat and it went along with them up the river. They marched on the east side of the river and met some soldiers and later some other soldiers with Arapahoes.[154] All of these were to meet and go with Custer against the Dakotas but it was now too late. As the Arapahoe Indians came near, the soldiers first took them for Dakotas and got ready to fight.[155] The Arapahoes

---

[154] They met Crook August 10th. — *Report of Secretary of War, 1876,* I, p. 466.

[155] This was true. Terry's scouts brought information that the Da-

told the scouts that the whole plan had been made for a battle after all the soldiers had assembled, but Custer had fought too soon.

Later Supplementary Story of Goes-Ahead, Crow Scout with Custer.

He put his name down with the others. The soldiers were encamped where still water flows into the Yellowstone. The grass was just coming up, and there was snow on the ground. The Indians called General Terry, No-Hip-bone. They went on to where Powder River joins the Yellowstone. They turned back and up the Yellowstone a little till the leaves began to come on the trees and the water was high. The buffalo began to get scarce and they knew that someone was hunting them (Dakotas and Cheyennes). The Crows were on the north side of the Yellowstone and the soldiers wanted to cross but it was too high. General Terry had a canoe. At Medicine Creek an infantry commander who had smallpox joined General Terry; they called him Porous Face. Then a steamboat came up the Yellowstone, opposite the mouth of the Rosebud. Some of the Crow scouts got on this boat and went across. Among those with Goes-Ahead were: Young Yellow Wolf, Long Crow, Spotted White Bird, a white man (Bonny Brave), interpreter, Bull Jack Rabbit, Shows-his-Face, Small Face, Dirty-Faced

kotas were in front of them and while preparations for attack were being made, Crook's couriers arrived and announced it was Crook's force that confronted Terry. — *Report of Secretary of War*, I, p. 466.

Coyote, Two Whistles, Grandmother's Knife, Heart Horse, Elk, Push, Throws-his-Ears, Buffalo Calf, Mountain, Coyote, White-Man-Runs-Him, Half-Yellow-Face, Curly, Hairy Moccasin, and White Swan.

The roll was called at the bank at the boat for these Crow scouts. Six of them were called to go on board, Hairy Moccasin, White-Man-Runs-Him, Goes-Ahead, Curly, Half-Yellow-Face, White Swan. The boat went up a little way and landed the scouts. Their interpreter was Mitch. Bouyer, (Ka-pēsh), a half-breed Dakota. He told them that when they went down below the mouth of the Rosebud they would see Arikara scouts.[156] When they came to this camp there was a big tent with a flag, and in it they met Custer. He shook hands with them and said, "We are glad to have you, we sent for you and you came right away." Custer had then hair down to his shoulders. He told them he was going to fight the Dakotas and Cheyennes and that he understood that the Crows were good scouts. "If we win the fight, everything belonging to the enemy you can take home, for my boys have no use for these things." The next day they broke camp and went up the Rosebud until night.[157] Next day they found where the Dakotas had their first camp, a very big one.[158] They had had a sun dance, they

---

[156] Mitch Bouyer was the guide and Crow interpreter. He was a half-breed. — Godfrey, *Custer's Last Battle*, p. 365.

[157] This was June 22d. — *Ib.*, p. 364.

[158] On June 23d. *Ib.*, p. 366.

could see the frame of the dance lodge.[159]   The third day they camped at what is now Busby School, the second camp on the Rosebud.   Just at dawn they reached Wolf Mountain, the sun was just coming up.   Custer always warned them to look out for themselves, for every squad of soldiers had scouts and they might be mistaken for the enemy.   Custer said to the six Crow scouts: "If nothing happens to me I will look after you in the future."   From Wolf Mountain the Crow scouts were ahead but stopped a moment at the lone tepee.   At White Rocks, Mitch Bouyer told them to go with Custer. As Custer swung off from the trail after Reno left him to cross the upper ford there was an Arikara scout and four Crow scouts with him.[160]   Custer rode to the edge of the high bank and looked over to the place where Reno's men were, as though planning the next move.   When they had arrived at about the point where Lieutenant Hodgson's headstone was placed later, the three Crow scouts saw the soldiers under Reno dismounting in front of the Dakota camp and thought that the enemy were "too many." Close to where Reno and Benteen later in the day were attacked by the Dakotas, on the ridge of hills above the river, the three Crow scouts were left behind and Custer's command went down the draw toward the lower ford on the run.   Custer had told

---

[159] It was June 24th that they found the "Sun-dance" lodge. — Godfrey, *Custer's Last Battle*, p. 366.

[160] The Crows were with Custer and remained with the command. — *Ib.*, p. 372.

the Crow scouts to stay out of the fight and they went to the left along the ridge overlooking the river while he took his command to the right (Goes-Ahead is sure Curly, the Crow scout, was not with him). At this point both Curly and (Black) Fox, Arikara scout, disappeared. Black Fox rode a bay horse and Curly rode a bald-faced pony with front white stockings and a D brand on the rump. The three Crow scouts rode along the high ridge, keeping back from the view of the Dakotas till they came to the end of the ridge and to the bluff just above the lower ford. There they dismounted and fired across into the Dakota camp, the circle of tents they could see over the tree-tops below them. They heard two volleys fired and saw the soldiers' horses standing back of the line in groups. Then in accordance with orders Custer had given them about staying out of the fight, they rode back along the ridge and met the Arikara scouts and pack-mules. They then rode away around the point of the highest hill, incorrectly called Custer's Last Look, and along the ridge. After riding all night they reached the mouth of the Little Big Horn by daylight. Here Terry met them. He asked about Custer and they told him Custer had been wiped out. He asked them four times.[161]

[161] Terry's scouts were sent out at 4 A.M. June 26th. "They soon discovered three Indians, who were at first supposed to be Sioux; but, when overtaken, they proved to be Crows, who had been with General Custer. They brought the first intelligence of the battle. Their story was not credited." — *Report of Secretary of War, 1876*, I, p. 463.

APPENDIX

STORY TOLD BY STRIKES TWO AND BEAR'S BELLY

OF AN EXPEDITION UNDER CUSTER TO THE BLACK HILLS IN JUNE, 1875

ALFRED BEAR, INTERPRETER

The scouts on the expedition were as follows: Bloody Knife and Lean Bear, as leaders; Bear's Ears, Horns-in-Front, Crow Bear, Standing Soldier, Standing, Red Horse, Bear's Arm, Strikes Two, Bear's Belly, Enemy Heart, Young Hawk, Red Bear, Little Sioux, Bear's Eyes, Left Hand (different in his discharge papers), Goose, Angry Bear (Mandan name, He-ra-ta-ke), Red Angry Bear, Crooked Horn (Arikara), Elk Face, Angry Bull (half Dakota and half Arikara), Left Hand (Dakota), Spotted Horse Eagle (Dakota), Shoots the Bear (Dakota), Two-Blackfoot, and twenty-five Santee scouts.

They started from their camp at the bottom of a hill on the present site of Mandan and joined Custer at his fort. They went south on the hill, crossing the Cannon Ball at the sacred stone or the stone with the holy writing on it. After two or three nights they camped at a place they called the cave or den. The Arikara were told by the Dakota scouts that they were near the big den or cave so that they camped and went to look for it. The walls were covered with painted designs and toward the interior were carved figures on the walls. On the ceiling a flash of lightning was figured.[1] The dung of deer covered all the floor to the opening into the interior. Here the ceiling was out of reach and it was wholly dark. At the opening of the interior were offerings of beads in a heap and bracelets. From here they picked up a flint-lock and took it to Custer. Beyond the cave were two piles of stones put up by the Dakotas and still farther on from the opening was a large flat rock. When they first found this cave they saw on the flat rock a woman taking the hair off a deer hide with an old-fashioned scraper. She ran away and they could not find her. They thought she hid in the cave, far in. Beyond the flat rock was a spring. Here was a large hollow rock full of water like a trough in a pasture and the tracks of the deer were all about like cow tracks at a watering place. The soldiers came after this to explore the cave. They had three candles and a pick and shovel. The Arikara scouts went in till the cave floor slanted steeply down and then they went back. The Mandan scout was with the soldiers and stayed after the other scouts left. But he turned back too after he was about half way

[1] The Lucky Man was the first to enter the cave, Enemy Heart was second and Red Nose, a white man, was third. The figures of all sorts of animals were carved on the rocks in the cave.

down. The next morning their interpreter for the Dakotas, Baker (his sons are Lewis and James), told them that the soldiers found it wet and muddy and had to turn back after going knee deep without reaching the end. The next morning they broke camp and came to a butte shining with selenite, and large pieces at the bottom. The next place was Black Butte, heavy cedar timber was all over it. Here Custer sent two scouts back with mail, Bull Neck and Skunk Head.

They now entered the timber, it looked like a prairie that had been burned, it was so black. They camped at a river, shallow like the Little Missouri. They called it the Big River and the Dakotas call it the Beautiful River. There was pine timber on both sides of the river. Across the river was the Cut Butte, with two high points, and they camped here. The scouts were on a hill and the soldiers were in a valley. Their interpreter told them that two soldiers were quarreling and one of them asked Custer for permission to finish the fight. Custer said, "I don't care," and one of the soldiers got his gun out. The scouts heard someone call, "Hold on, hold on," and then a shot, and then another. The soldier shot his comrade through the arm and then through the heart. The dead body was carried on in a wagon. Custer came to the scouts and told them that the doctor was planning to cut up the body to see why he was so quarrelsome. The scouts saw the doctor cut the body open, put salt in the body, put all the parts back and then the body was buried. The soldiers fired a salute over the grave. The next morning they set out through the timber and they tried to keep track of the number of days they were in the woods. When they came to a butte they went up and saw only timber, no earth at all. They found an old Dakota camp where they had been preparing tepee poles, peeling bark and leaning the poles up on trees near by. The camp was old but presently they struck a fresh Dakota trail. Custer told them to go on duty and a few scouts went ahead to scout. A fresh Dakota camp was reported by the scouts and they all went on to the place and found coals of fire not yet out, deer bones freshly gnawed, dried meat still hanging here and there. All the scouts lined up under Custer's orders and he picked out the best of them to scout ahead to look for the Dakota camp. Strikes Two was one of these and two white men, soldiers, not officers. At a place where there was a junction of two ravines they saw at their right up the ravine the Dakota camp. There were five tepees and it was as far as from Bear's Belly's house to Red Bear's house. They sent the two white soldiers back to Custer to notify him. They stood together at the top of the hill and looked across the ravine. They could hear scattered shots from the Dakota hunters. The soldiers came up and Custer sent one party of scouts to surround the camp and the others were to charge straight in. Strikes Two was with the first party and Bear's Belly was with the second. The first party surrounded the camp and waited for the others to charge. Then they heard the horses charging in and they ran out of the woods. They saw two boys with a yellow blanket on and they were afraid and cried and ran up where there was a creek. They threw away their blanket and the scouts saw the fish they had. Then a naked warrior ran out with a gun which he held up against the charging scouts. Red Angry Bear reached him first and struck him with his whip and the others did the same. The women ran out and tried to get away into the woods but the scouts told them to go to their tents. They found out the warrior's gun had no hammer and he was the only man there. Then he went inside and came out with a pipe which he held towards the scouts as a peace sign. Custer then came up with his men and called up the Dakota scouts and they told Custer that the camp would follow as they were prisoners. He left one white man in the camp to see that they came on and one white man on a hill to watch them. When three Dakota hunters came back they told the man in camp they were going to buy a gun of the soldiers so he went with them to the other white soldier and they all came on to Custer's camp. One Dakota came to where the scouts were and by signs told them that he wanted to get a gun in exchange for a horse. He said he would go and get his horse and Custer said, all right, but told the

other two to stay behind. The other Dakota scouts
went along with the Dakota captives but one lagged
back and ran away to a creek. Then they saw the
other Dakota wrestling on horseback with his cap-
tor. The Dakota scout drew his revolver and fired
but the two Dakotas got away. The Arikara scouts
fired one shot apiece and the Dakota scouts held one
of the Dakota captives, the old man. They all rode
on to the old camp but all the Dakotas were gone.
They followed hard on the trail till dark and then
gave it up.

They returned and found the old Dakota tied
outside to an iron picket pin. His feet were hob-
bled, he had a string around his waist and his leg
was bandaged but his hands were not tied. Custer
came to the Arikara and made signs that he at first
planned to have them kill this Dakota captive but
that now he was to be guide. The captive tried to
tell them that they were coming to more Dakotas
than their whole number and all would be killed.
At last they came to the Shell River (Shell as breast
plate, Arikara name). Here the Dakota guide
pointed out distant smoke on the prairie and said
it was a train and a town. Custer said he was to
stop and give up and return on the back trail. The
officer the Arikara called the Lucky Man (Charley Reynolds), was given papers by Custer and he
went on alone. He was a good hunter and a dead
shot. He was to go to the town in the direction of
the smoke. The Dakota captive cried in the night

and by signs said that his children would cut their hair as for his death since he was as good as dead. At one place Custer signed to the scouts that he proposed to let the Dakota captive go. He gave the Dakota a good suit, hat, and other things, and though the Arikara planned to kill him, Custer got him off in the night and they never saw him again.

From this they camped at a broken place. Red Angry Bear found some gold in a spring and word was sent in the Arikara language that they were all to come and get some of the pretty yellow stuff to trim their bridles with. They all got some and their arms were sparkling with the golden dust. Custer asked them where they got the gold and they showed him. He sounded a bugle and called the soldiers and put pickets out to keep all others away. Then Custer came with some gold in a cloth and opened it before the Arikara saying, "You scouts have found this which is money and you shall have your share," as he said this he picked up and threw down gold by handfuls, "You shall have it like this," he said. The soldiers had gotten this gold from the spring, digging where the Indians had first found it. He said this land would be marked and it was marked so they could find it again. Piles of stones were put up and the soldiers went about putting up marks or signs. They marched to the Bear Butte and six scouts were sent with mail to Fort Lincoln. Three of these were Arikara scouts, Strikes Two, Angry Bear, and Left Hand. The other three were Dakota scouts, one of them was called Goose. Strikes Two had a horse with mailbags and Custer gave him a flask of whiskey. They rode off at sunset and rode all night and after a rest they rode on all day and reached the Beautiful River. After crossing the river they traveled one-half the night and all day. They took six days to get to Fort Lincoln. They were here a day when the Lucky Man got in. He had delivered his papers and had come on to Fort Lincoln by rail. After twelve days Custer's party came in.

F. F. GERARD'S STORY OF THE CUSTER FIGHT [1]

On June 22d, Custer's command left the mouth of the Rosebud looking for Indians. On June 24th, we broke camp and marched all day and in evening went into camp. The men had supper and grazed their horses and then marched all night till 4 A. M., when a halt was called. The horses remained saddled but the soldiers slept on the ground as best they could. Two Arikara scouts arrived from Lieutenant Varnum, who had been sent out to reconnoitre and locate Indian camps. They brought word of a very large camp down in Little Big Horn Valley, but the Indians had discovered us and were on the run. Custer ordered me to go with him and the two Arikara scouts who had come in from Varnum and two of our scouts, to where Lieutenant Varnum was. About daybreak we reached Varnum and could see the large black mass moving in front and down the Little Big Horn and a dense cloud of dust over all and behind. The camp we had found was the smaller camp (the larger camp was downstream farther), and was on the way to the larger camp and this led us all to believe that the Indians were stampeded. Custer and his party with Varnum

---

1 From a personal interview with Gerard. [ED.]

and his scouts started back to rejoin the command
at a sharp gait. Before reaching his troops, about
half way back, Tom Custer met us at the head of
the troops and Custer addressed him saying: "Tom,
who in the devil moved these troops forward? My
orders and intentions were to remain in camp all
day and make a night attack on the Indians but
they have discovered us and are on the run." After joining the troops, Custer with his officers held
a consultation and decided it would be better to follow the Indians so he divided his command into
three battalions, one under his own command, Benteen in command of the second, and Reno of the
third. Benteen he sent to the left of the command
to overlook the ridges as we marched down the valley. He then ordered Reno to take his command
and try to overtake the Indians and bring them to
battle while he himself would support him. Custer
said: "Take the scouts with you." Reno started on
the double quick down the valley until he came to
the Little Big Horn. Up to that time we were all
still under the impression that the Indians were
running away. Upon reaching the ford of the
Little Big Horn, I discovered that the Indians
were coming back to give us battle and called Reno's attention to this change in their movements.
Reno halted for a few seconds and ordered the men
forward. Thinking that Custer should know of
this change of front on the part of the Indians, I
rode back at once to tell Custer the news. At an

abrupt turn I met Cook, Custer's adjutant, ahead of his command, who said: "Gerard, what's up?" On hearing the news he ordered me back to Reno's command and rode to inform Custer of the change in the front on the part of the Indians. I rejoined Reno's command just as he was drawing up his men on the skirmish line. The men were almost six feet apart along the brow of a hill below which was a belt of timber. As the Indians came charging back the men used the timber for cover and the Indians rode by on the left and around to the higher ground at the rear and left. Not more than four rounds had been fired before they saw Custer's command dashing along the hills one mile to their rear. Reno then gave the order: "The Indians are taking us in the rear, mount and charge." This was then about 1:30 P.M. I was surprised at this change of position as we had excellent cover and could hold off the Indians indefinitely, but the orders were to mount and charge. Charley Reynolds was killed as he rode up the slope at the left and Isaiah a little farther out. Reno led his men in Indian file back to the ford above which he had seen Custer's command pass. The Indians picked off the troops at will; it was a rout not a charge. All the men were shot in the back, some men fell before high ground was reached. As soon as the hill was gained, Benteen and his command came up and the demoralization of Reno's men affected his own men and no attempt was made to go to Custer's aid. They remained where they were though it was about 2 P.M. and no Indians attacked them for more than an hour.

After Reno's command left, I found in the timber Lieutenant de Rudio, Sergeant O'Neill and Wm. Jackson, a half-breed Blackfoot scout, who were also cut off from the command. All the afternoon we could hear the troop volleys, but the scattering fire of the Indians gradually predominated till we were sure that the Indians had won. The fight where Reno's men were began shortly after 4 and kept up till dark. We remained where we were till dark and then struck out west thinking Reno's command had returned. We missed the morning ford and tried the ford Reno used to retreat by but the dead bodies made the horses snort and the water looked too deep so they returned and found a new ford. As we mounted the bank we saw a match lit and called out: "There are the troops, Hello!" and then the match was put out. As we neared the old crossing we saw the Indian lances against the sky and the Indians hearing us turn off suddenly, called out, "Are you afraid, we are not white troops." De Rudio and O'Neill lay down and hid in the brush at this point while Jackson and I rode down and across the stream straight against a cut bank. Both horses threw their riders, our guns were lost, but finally a ford was found and just at dawn we rode out on the prairie. At the left we could hear more

Indians coming across the Little Big Horn, coming down to attack Reno. Then we galloped hard to the bunch of willows at the right and reached it before the Indians came out of the water. Here we remained till dark. About 11 A. M. we saw them attack Reno's camp. About one hour before sunset a great talking and confusion arose, the Indians evidently saw Terry coming and began to fall back. Some left for their village to gather their families while others rode away up the Little Big Horn. The retreating warriors passed by hundreds close to where we lay hid in the willows.

BIOGRAPHIES

BIOGRAPHIES

SOLDIER

Soldier was born in 1831. His people lived in the Arikara village next to the timber on the Missouri River. The chief of the village was then Dog Chief. The other village was called the village of the Easterners. His village was across the coulee from this one. Both villages were on the west side of the Missouri River (Grand River villages). Soldier was born in a winter camp, late in the fall, on the day when the Arikara and the Yanktonnais fought. Some of their houses were still incomplete, not yet being covered over with earth. The following spring One Feather was born on the journey of the tribe to the Pawnee country. Both villages were on their way down to the Pawnees in 1832. They remained with this tribe three winters. The land of the Pawnees was called the country of the Broad River. Soldier was then four years old and he remembers that on their return one camp was made late in the fall because there was snow on the ground.

On this journey he saw a party of white men. They had long yellow hair, wore mustaches, carried guns and bows and arrows, were dressed like Indians, and rode horses. They had fine blankets and different kinds of corn and the Arikara traded robes for the corn. Some of the robes that the Arikara had for trade were decorated with the sign of the cross. He remembers that the white men gave very much more corn for these robes for they said the cross was a holy sign that should be used only at death. The Indians and whites held a council and the whites said many more of their kind were coming to the Indian country and they would not let Arikara have their medicine but they would use it only to kill their enemies. The traders told the Arikara that they were their friends and would not sell their medicine to the many whites who were coming in, for the settlers would distribute it and kill many Indians. These traders came from the south. Soldier remembers the camp caller going about among the tents repeating the words of the traders regarding their medicine. This took place in the Black Hills country, and he remembers seeing here a large upright stone. The Arikara pushed on toward the Missouri River and they met before leaving it, the war party that had left them and they had three prisoners, people who lived in grass houses beyond the Crow Indians and the Black Hills country. These prisoners were two women and one boy. One of the women was named by them the Grass House Woman. The boy was called Yellow Bird, and the other woman, daughter of the first, later married a white man, a laborer.

This white man had come up the Missouri River in a row boat and he took his wife back down the river with him.

Late in the fall the Arikara arrived at Painted Butte across the Yellowstone. Here they wintered and in the spring they returned to the Missouri and spent the summer hunting with the Hidatsa at the Five Villages. There were two Hidatsa villages on opposite sides of the Knife River, or as they called it, Branching Creek. In the fall of 1837 they left the Hidatsa and made a winter camp on the west side of the Missouri River near Washburn. Here they were attacked by the smallpox and many of them died. Soldier was living at this time with his parents at the Antelope, or Upper Village of the Mandans. The smallpox spread from the Arikara camp to this village of the Mandans and here both of his parents and his sister died of the disease. After this Soldier was taken to the lower or larger (Fort Clark) Mandan village by his grandmother, his mother's mother, Skunk Woman. Here he had the smallpox when he was just six years old. To escape the smallpox many of the Arikara and Mandans went up the river and a number of them died on the way and the bodies were left behind them on the trail.

At the Fort Clark Village Soldier lived twenty-four years. Near this village on a little creek there was a trading post. The Indians called the trader Big Knife, and Soldier remembers him as short, slender, and good looking. The same year the trader married an Arikara wife, Lucky Woman, daughter of Star and sister of Son-of-Star. At this same place there was a white doctor and he vaccinated some of the Indians, among them Sitting Bear and all of his sisters (children of Son-of-Star), and Chief Woman, Young Hawk's wife. Gerard was interpreter for the doctor. That same year, 1837, a steamboat was reported going up the river and it landed near the village. There were other white men here also.

Soldier married an Arikara woman when he was twenty years old, and their two children died long after at Fort Berthold of the smallpox. The trader, Big Knife, died at Fort Clark and was buried there. The next trader was Dawson, but the Indians called him Big Knife also. His son, Bear's Arm, and his daughter, Anne Snow, are both still living.

After Dawson, Gerard was the next trader at Fort Clark. A short distance up the river there was at this time an Hidatsa village. In 1838, the trading post was abandoned and the traders moved up to Fort Berthold. Soldier remembers that the cause of the abandonment of the Fort Clark trading post was a quarrel between the Dakotas and Gerard's clerk, and that the Arikara sided with the traders. Soldier saw the traders get on their loaded boats and go up the river to Fort Berthold, and the same year the Arikara were invited by the Hidatsa to come up the river. For some time after this the Arikara had to go up to the post to get supplies and it was very inconvenient. Some time later the Arikara moved up the Missouri River and camped near Expansion. The next day they moved over to Fort Berthold. This was before the building of the two Arikara villages opposite Fort Berthold. White Shield led this band of Arikara and Soldier lived here in a roundhouse until the village broke up.

He remembers seeing a miner's boat with some men, one woman, and two children come down the river. One of the men had a long beard and they all landed and made a fire on the bank and then went up to Gerard's store where they stayed for the night. This was the same year that the soldiers fought the Dakotas at Bismarck (Sibley's Expedition, 1863). Gerard told the Arikara that he tried to make the men in the boat stay six or seven days till the Dakotas got across and away from the Missouri River, but the leader of the whites, the man with the beard, said they would go right on. Afterwards the Arikara reported that they had heard shots down the river and they told Gerard. He sent Soldier and Howling Bear to go down the river and find the boat. He told them that the gold was in skin sacks in each end of the boat. "If you find the boat," he said, "look in the end, there is a little door, and there is the gold. If the Dakotas find the gold they will throw it away for they do not know what it is." Some of the other Arikara heard that Soldier was going and Red Bear (not the present one), Bull Head, and Bull Neck came in and said that they were going too. One other Indian went also. They went down the west side of the river for they were afraid of the Dakotas. Gerard gave them a nugget of gold so they would know what to look for. He promised the two Arikara that if they found the gold, Howling Bear could have the best horse he had and Soldier could go to his store twice and pick out what he wanted.

When they crossed the Knife River they killed one of a herd of buffalo for food. Here they stayed all night. The next morning they started on foot and camped near the mouth of Heart River. Then they went toward the Missouri and saw many horse tracks. On the other side of the river they saw a small log raft which the Dakotas had probably used in crossing. They put their clothing and guns on a raft and crossed by pushing and pulling it. On the other side they found many of the rafts used by the Dakotas. They left their clothes on the raft and took their guns. Soldier and the other Indian stayed behind. Presently they heard the others call that they saw dead bodies on a sand-bar. The bodies were naked and looked white as paper. They lay about one and one-half miles upstream from where the Northern Pacific bridge now stands. The current ran on the west side and the bodies lay on the lower end of the long sand-bar with the slack water between them and the east bank. As Soldier came down the bank he saw holes in the river sand on the side where the Dakotas had thrown up breastworks. One was large enough for four or five persons, the others would hold only one. Out on the sand-bar upstream from the dead bodies, he saw in the largest rifle pit an empty coffee-pot and something that showed yellow when the wind blew the sand up. He called Howling Bear, who had one of the gold nuggets Gerard had given them, and with this they concluded that they had found the gold, but Howling Bear said nothing, he simply gathered up the gold into a coffee-pot. Where they found the gold, the Dakotas had cut open the sacks and poured the gold out in a heap on the sand. Afterwards Howling Bear cleaned the gold by holding it in a shallow pan in the swift current of the river. After Howling Bear left the place, the other Indians came and dug and got a little in their own hands, but Howling Bear persuaded them to put it all in his sack. The Indians took turns in carrying the gold back to Fort Berthold. They put it all into one sack about twelve inches long and Soldier remembers that it weighed about as much as a sack of flour. All this gold they gave to Gerard as he was the only trader at the fort.

After gathering up the gold they all went over and looked at the bodies of the white men. They were slashed with knives but not scalped. There were nine or ten of them all thrown together and Soldier judged that they had been dead about five days. They saw just the top of a tepee in the timber on the east bank of the river and heard afterwards that it contained the body of a Dakota killed in the fight with the white men.

Soldier was a member of various secret societies of his tribe, passing from one to the other as he grew older. Among them were the Crow Society, Foolish Dog Society, Black Mouth Society, and last of all the Buffalo Society, of which he is still a member. In 1904 he was made chief by the Arikara and he was presented with a chief's war shirt by Dog's Backbone, who had resigned. The latter had received his chief's war shirt from the former chief, Soup. Bear's Teeth, Strikes Two, Standing Soldier, and Sitting Bear are the other Arikara chiefs who are entitled to wear these shirts.

While he was on a hunting trip about 1854, many Dakotas chased the party into the woods near Dickinson, on a creek running north. Many of the Arikara were killed and Soldier was shot clear through the upper chest on the right side. Many other Arikara were wounded and the ten who were killed were buried in the ground. With the party were also Mandans and Hidatsa and one trader, grandfather of Peter Beauchamp. The trader on this hunting trip had a wagon which was abandoned on the chase and the wheels were chopped to pieces by the Dakotas. Soldier was so badly wounded that he made part of the return trip on a travois.

Soldier's family: Grandfather, He-Holds-the-

Enemy-Back; father, Bear's Arm, born about 1767, died at Fort Clark, 1837; mother, Assiniboine Woman, born about 1787, died, 1837; uncles, Many Bears and Angry Horse; brother, Good Day.

STRIKES TWO

Strikes Two was born in 1844 at Fort Clark Village. His father was Arikara Chief and his mother was Young-Woman-Village. His father's father was Holding Medicine, and his mother's father was Old Elk. His father's mother was People-They-Know-Her, and his mother's mother was Old-Woman-Mist. His mother died of cholera (1851?) and his father died at Fort Berthold in 1901.

They left Fort Clark in the fall of 1861 and wintered in two parties, one four miles from Bear's Belly and one just below William Fighting Bear's place in the bottom and farther up the stream. The lower camp was without a head, for all the chiefs were in the upper camp, where there were also some Mandans and some Hidatsa. Before the ice broke in the spring, all the Arikara moved down the river and built two villages across from Fort Berthold. In the fall of the same year they crossed the river and joined the Fort Berthold Village, after they had been attacked by the Dakotas, who camped near their villages, to trade for corn. That winter they all camped at L'eau Qui Monte with a few Assiniboines. This was the year the Dakotas attacked Fort Berthold and were beaten off by Gerard and his white men, Pierre Garreau, Dawson's son, Hair-on-Upper-Lip, one mulatto, and the following Arikara, Hidatsa, and Mandans, who remained there without their families:

Arikara: Black Road, One-Horn-Wandering, Paint, White-Face-Bear, Young Fox, Bull Neck, Strikes Enemy, Rough Horn, Spotted Horse, Weasel Tail, He Hawk, Bull Head, Stabbed.

Hidatsa: Snake Cane, Hay Wolf, Hard Horn, Pan, Many Bears (he took the news to L'eau Qui Monte), Pointed Knife.

Mandans: White Bear, Leggings, Bald-Headed Eagle, Bad Gun.

One day Many Bears and Strikes Enemy were trying to sneak up on a herd of antelope near the present graveyard at Fort Berthold. Strikes Enemy saw the Dakotas coming, and ran back without telling Many Bears, who escaped the Dakotas and gave the alarm to the camp at L'eau Qui Monte. The whole camp then moved back to Fort Berthold and remained the rest of the winter.

In 1872, Howling Bear, an Arikara and chief of the scouts at Fort Lincoln, rode to Fort Berthold for recruits. He went to the lodge of Son-of-Star and told him what he wanted. The chief called a feast and Howling Bear made a speech for volunteers. Sitting Bull and Picketed offered themselves as leaders and Howling Bear left these two Arikara to recruit at Fort Berthold and went back to Fort Lincoln. The third leader was Lean Bear, and the other scouts were Strikes Two, Enemy Heart, Bull Neck, Four Rings, Elk Face, White Eagle, Skunk, Paint, Afraid-of-No-One, Pretty Crow, Elk Tongue, Wolf Looking, Buffalo, Bull-Walking-Through-Village, Bravest Man, Skunk Head.

This was in the fall, either in September or October. They went in bull-boats down to Fort Lincoln on the hill. They took in their boats corn balls, ears of corn, guns, and blankets. They hunted on the way down and the trip took three days. When they arrived they found that the Dakotas had attacked the fort four days before and had killed five Arikara. They were shown where their comrades had been killed for they had all lain close together and the blood was dried and cracked in the sun. Red Bear and Paint had gone out on duty in the morning and the Dakotas had attacked them suddenly. Red Bear was overtaken and killed but Paint got back to the fort. Boy Chief then rushed out to avenge his father's death and was killed close to his body. The other Arikara killed were Crow Tail, Spotted Eagle, and Ree-Standing-among-the-Hidatsa.

When the scouts from Fort Berthold reported for duty their commander told them they were to be examined the next day. Early the next morning they went out on foot to look for the Dakotas. Red Wolf overtook Strikes Two and gave him his horse. Strikes Two rode out with a few others who had borrowed horses from the older scouts. The Dakotas met them and killed Strikes Two's horse and one of them dashed up and struck the horse. Then Strikes Two got behind some rocks and shot at the Dakotas. He was wounded in the right leg just above the knee by a bullet from a shell loaded by a Dakota. Standing Soldier (Young War Eagle) put him on his own horse and took him back to camp. Elk Tongue and Wolf Looking, two Arikara scouts, who were fighting on foot, were killed. When the white soldiers saw the Arikara fall back, they went out and drove off the Dakotas.

Strikes Two's wound was first cared for in camp by three Arikara women, Fighting (War) Woman, White Woman, wife of a soldier, and the wife of Bear's Arm. War Woman took part in the fight at the fort after Red Bear was killed. She lived by herself and she was the mother of Bull, companion of Red Star during the Custer campaign of 1876. She lived at the camp and did work among the soldiers. Her son, too young at first to scout, lived with her. Bear's Arm was her nephew. War Woman and White Basket Woman helped Strikes Two to cut the bullet out of his leg. The doctor advised that the leg be cut off but the other Arikara did not like this and they sent him home on horseback. All the new recruits went back with him. He had to camp often on account of his wound and all winter he limped about on canes.

Strikes Two was married in 1876 after his return from service, and his wife is still living with him after thirty-six years. He did not reënlist as a scout. Chief Scab-on-Eye was one of the agents at Fort Berthold and the scouts afterwards saw him on the Powder River as an officer of the infantry.

LITTLE SIOUX

Little Sioux (One Wolf, earlier name), was born at Fort Clark, in 1857. His father was Small Brave, a Dakota, and his mother, Young Holy Woman, an Arikara. His grandfather, his mother's father, was Black Crow, and his grandmother was an Arikara. He remembers the white trader at Fort Clark, Going-on-side; he was a half-breed Pawnee. He was trading in opposition to F. F. Gerard and his trading post was a short distance north of the Fort Clark Village. Little Sioux was four years old when the Arikara came up to Fort Berthold from Fort Clark in the fall of 1861, and the tribe wintered down the river from Heart Camp, four miles above the present home of Bear's Belly.

He was young when his father died, but old enough to work at the time of his mother's death. They both died at Fort Berthold, where they lived in a round house. His brother was Red Wolf (Red Brush) and his two sisters were Young-Calf-Woman and Young-Bird-Woman. He was married in 1874 at the age of eighteen to his first wife, Young-Big-Horn-Woman.

In 1875, both he and his brother enlisted at Fort

Lincoln on the hill. After the Custer fight, his time expired and he went up the river on a steamboat as hunter with the Northern Pacific survey. There were at this time but a few soldiers at Fort Lincoln. The surveyors began work at the Yellowstone and they met the graders at Taylor, east of Dickinson. Little Sioux was gone all summer and was back by winter. He received for the season's work $160, besides board and lodging. There was one other Arikara hunter with him, Charging-up-the-Hill. The total number of animals he killed was one hundred five, mostly black-tailed deer. Among them was one buffalo, a few antelope, and five or six mountain sheep. Charging-up-the-Hill killed one hundred six. They brought the game in on pack-mules.

When these two hunters returned in the fall they went out again with a party of twelve white men who were getting deer to ship east. With the party were two hunters on horseback, and the rest carried the camp outfit in three sleds drawn by horses. They went up the Heart River from Mandan and were gone three weeks. All of the game was shipped from Mandan. Little Sioux killed six deer and Charging-up-the-Hill killed nine. They received $25 a month for their work.

The next summer Little Sioux was mail carrier on the route from Fort Berthold to Fort Yates. On the trip he crossed the river by ferry at Fort Lincoln and stopped at Fort Rice. It took two days to make the entire trip, which included the regular stop at Fort Lincoln. He carried mail from 1878 to 1882, received $25 per month, and rode his own pony. He received besides this, feed for his horse and drew regular rations from the government. He used to stop at Joseph Taylor's woodyard, for Taylor could talk Pawnee. Near Pretty Buttes lived Long Feet and his wife, and Little Sioux stopped there sometimes. A wood-chopper named George lived above Joseph Taylor's place, the Arikara called him Humped-Back.

In 1882 Stabbed was hunting in the Little Missouri Bad Lands with a party. He went out after dark to look after the horses and a Dakota shot him and ran off all the horses. At this time Little Sioux was at Fort Lincoln and saw the white soldiers leave it. When he heard of his uncle's (Stabbed) death he went at once to Fort Berthold. The murder was reported to the agent at Fort Berthold, an old man they called Soft Neck, and the Dakotas and the horses were finally located on the Rosebud in South Dakota. The next summer an equal number of horses were returned for at this time the government did not allow the Indians to make war on each other or to steal horses. The traders at Fort Berthold were called White-Man-Who-Talks-Sioux and Big Nose.

YOUNG HAWK

Young Hawk was born in the spring of 1859 at the winter village of the Arikara just below Mannhaven. His father, Forked Horn, was a Custer scout and died in 1894. He was born about 1815. His mother, Red-Corn-Silk-Woman, was born in 1835 and died in 1911. Her father was Wolf-Skin-Arrow-Sheath and her mother was named Eagle. Young Hawk's early name was Striped Horn, then Crazy Head; Young Hawk was his uncle's name. This uncle was a very brave man and when Young Hawk first enlisted at Fort Lincoln, his father had his name changed to Young Hawk. At the time Red Bear's father was killed, Young Hawk was present and fought. He was then only thirteen years old and he was not an enlisted scout, but his father was so proud of him that he named him Young Hawk. He was on the Black Hills Expedition with Custer.

On this trip Charley Reynolds and Bloody Knife were scouting the trail and the wagons got stuck at a high cut-bank where there were many trees. Custer asked whose fault it was and Reynolds said, "Bloody Knife's." Then Custer drew a revolver and shot at them several times, and they saved themselves by dodging behind trees. When Custer put up his pistol, Bloody Knife came to where he sat on his horse and said, "It is not a good thing you have done to me; if I had been possessed of madness, too, you would not see another day." Custer replied, "My brother, it was the madness of a moment that made me do this, but it is gone now. Let us shake hands and be friends again." So Bloody Knife agreed and they shook hands.

On another occasion, during Custer's march from Fort Lincoln to the Yellowstone in 1876, Custer had ridden ahead with a scout in search of a trail. When the rest of the command reached a place where the roads forked, no one knew which way Custer had gone. Some one asked Custer's negro servant, Isa, which road to take and he chose the fork of the road in the other direction from the one taken by Custer because it was a very good road. When Custer and his scout returned he found that the whole command had not halted but had taken the other road. Red Star was at some distance scouting among the hills, but as he rode into camp he saw Isa on his knees before Custer, who was cursing him furiously, while the darky was crying and begging for mercy. The next day as a punishment Isa had to go on foot all day.

RED STAR

Red Star (Strikes the Bear) was born in 1858 at Fort Clark. His father, also Red Star, was born at Fort Clark in 1828 and died at the same place in 1860 or early in 1861. His mother, Woman-Goes-Into-Every-House, was born at Fort Clark in 1831 and was killed with her five-year-old daughter by the Dakotas at the Arikara village opposite Fort Berthold. When the Arikara village at Grand River was fired upon by soldiers using cannon in 1828, some of the Arikara went down to the Pawnees and some went up to the Mandan village at

Fort Clark. The family of Red Star's mother went north; her father's name was Man-That-Drives-Horses-Away. Red Star's foster grandfather was Big Star, who was born at the Cannon Ball village, the one the soldiers fired upon. His grandfather, White Geese, was son of Star, and the father of Big Star was Looking-for-Kettle. His older brother, Red Willow, about ten years older than Red Star, died when fifteen years old at Fort Berthold. His sister, Owl Woman, was eight years younger than Red Star. She died at Fort Berthold at the age of twelve. The three children went to their grandmother, Spotted-Corn-Stalk, and his father's sister, Omaha Woman, whose husband was Sweat or Little Bear.

Red Star began to look after his uncle's horses when he was about nine years of age. At night the horses were kept in the front part of the lodge, twenty-five or thirty of them, tied to the rail at the right or left of the door, and one-fourth the way around the circle of the house. The women cut grass or bark of young cottonwood limbs and twigs in May, June, and July to feed the horses in the lodge. Red Star slept on a scaffold of four poles built two feet from the ground. The bottom of the bed was made of round willow poles laid crosswise, interlaced lengthwise by three willows and the whole was firmly bound together with rawhide. He had a bear-skin robe under him and a buffalo robe for cover.

Red Star's government record began when he was eighteen years old. When Boy Chief and Goose brought up the letter from Fort Lincoln asking for more scouts, Red Star went along with a group to serve. In this group were Young Hawk, Running Wolf, Strikes-the-Lodge, Charging Bull, Little Brave, Stabbed, Howling Wolf, One Horn, One Feather, Bull-in-the-Water, Tall Bear, and Strikes Two.

At Fort Lincoln they found Bloody Knife, Soldier, Bob-tailed Bull, No Heart, Bear, Red Wolf, Buffalo, Curly Head, and Owl. Red Star got his outfit and took the oath like the rest. They camped near the soldiers. At Bismarck they saw a few little houses and some stores but he saw no soldiers, only the buildings where the soldiers had been. They crossed the river on a steamboat. He had never been on a boat before. Here orders were given them for a day and a night by an officer. Gerard was their interpreter. This officer in charge of the Arikara scouts was Peaked Face (Lieutenant Varnum), and his orderlies were Bloody Knife and Bob-tailed Bull. They received their orders standing in line. Bloody Knife stood by Varnum at this time and Bob-tailed Bull stood in line with the rest of the scouts. Their first order was that a man who did not get up was to go without his breakfast. The scout who did not help the cook by getting water and wood when called upon was to go without meals. The scout who got drunk was punished by losing his horse and by being compelled to go on foot. Forked Horn and Black Fox volunteered to cook and the Indians chose them for that work. The cooks were not to go on scout. If the cook did not get up at call then someone else was to take his place. The guards called the cooks in the morning. As sentinels three of the scouts were detailed to go to the highest points as long as they were in camp but at night one of these sentinels was to come down and guard the horses and the other two remained at their post. Scouts on night duty did not come in until noon of the next day. All the scouts were inspected by an officer early each morning and anyone found asleep was compelled to go on foot during that day's march. Gerard told the scouts that they did not need to drill. Roll was called at night just before bed-time. On the march, the roll call was always taken on horseback, and the Arikara were not satisfied until they learned the reason why.

Red Star was on police duty for three years, from 1898 to 1901. His name was changed from Strikes-the-Bear to Red Star at the advice of Big Star, after the Custer campaign. Paint was the name of the man who performed the ceremony of giving him his new name. Red Bear got his father's name at the same time. Part of the ceremony was the offering of sacrifices and gifts to Mother Corn and these were afterwards given to the singers in the sacred lodge.

One fall Red Star and Bear's Belly went out hunting bear. They tracked one bear to the river and across the sand up to a cut bank cave. They went to the entrance and looked in but could see nothing. Then Red Star took a stick and poked about and at last felt the bear but could not stir him. Bear's Belly went up the bank to the other entrance and seeing the bear's head shot at him. He sank out of sight and the two men crawled into the den about eight feet and began poking about to find whether the bear was dead or alive. At last they found him dead, and Bear's Belly and Red Star had hard work dragging the bear out of the cave for he was large and very heavy. Bear's Belly took the head and skin to use in a ceremonial dance. In order to use this skin he was compelled to drag it home by means of thongs fastened to his own flesh. Red Star cut two gashes in Bear's Belly's back and fastened the rawhide thongs as is done in the sun dance. Red Star went on ahead after doing this for his companion and left him to drag the hide painfully the whole way home. When Red Star reached camp with the load of bear's fat he told the old men that Bear's Belly was dragging the hide and head into camp, and several of them went out to help him whenever his load caught on the edges of the cut banks over which he had to drag it. They did not come into the camp till the next day.

One day a bear's cub was brought into the Arikara village by a hunter. It tried to get milk from a woman but she did not know what it wanted and drove it away. Then at last a woman came into camp with a nursing boy and the cub went to her and pulled her dress with its claws, and she guessed what it wanted. She nursed him with the boy. The boy is now Yellow Bird. The bear grew up and was sold down the river on a boat.

A man rode first in a buffalo hunt and was first to fire at a buffalo while the other Indians waited for him. The buffalo turned quickly and charged and threw the man off his horse by catching him with his horns. The buffalo then turned and catching the man again tossed him into the air. The horse was standing close by waiting for the man to mount. The buffalo tried to gore the man but the horse sprang at him and caught him with his teeth near the ear and the two animals then fought, the horse biting and striking with his fore feet. At last the buffalo got clear and killed the horse with his horns. The man was saved and they kept the head of the horse in the village because it was unusual for a horse to attack a buffalo to save his master.

Red Bear

Red Bear was born at Fort Clark in September, 1853. His father, Red Bear (Red Man), was killed in 1872 at the Fort Lincoln fight described by Strikes Two. He was born in 1793 among the Pawnee. His mother, White Corn, was born in

1837 at Rock Village, a mile above the present town of Expansion on the Missouri River. His grandfather, Red Man's father, was Bear Above. His grandfather, White Corn's father, was a white man, a trader at Rock Village. His grandmother, Red Man's mother, was Yellow and she died at Rock Village. His grandmother, White Corn's mother, was Pretty-Stalk-of-Corn, who died at Fort Berthold when it was still a village, about the breaking up time.

Red Bear's early name was Handsome Elk, given him by Chief Owl, at his father's request so that he might live a long time and become famous. His father gave Chief Owl two large buffalo robes and a pile of dried meat. Then according to tribal ceremony the old man took the boy up on his own lodge in view of all the village when he was about six years old, and had the boy hold upright his scalp stick upon which hung an enemy's scalp. Then Chief Owl prayed to all the gods and last of all to the Great Spirit, that the boy might grow to be a good and brave man. He called to the boy to grow up brave and get a scalp and fight for him, his godfather. Then he pressed the boy's two feet together and down on the ground by taking hold of his ankles. Next he pressed his shoulders down, then his head with one hand, and finally he passed his hand upward from the boy's feet to his head, meaning for him to grow up a good man. Then he called upon all the people to witness that the boy was to be called Handsome Elk. The sun was near the horizon when the ceremony was completed, and the old man stood facing it. It was still and his voice carried far to all the listening village. This was a special ceremony performed only for the children of leading men.

Immediately after his father's death, Red Bear passed through the sun-dance torture in order to be his father's representative. He enlisted at Fort Stevenson in 1872 but returned home on account of sore eyes. His second enlistment was at Fort Lincoln, already described in the narrative. At Fort Stevenson there enlisted with him Yellow Horse, Red Chief, Little Soldier, and Little Brave. At the time of these enlistments the barracks at Fort Stevenson were just completed. He enlisted at his father's request, and his half-brother, Boy Chief, had already been taken to Fort Lincoln by his father.

He married Shell Woman in 1876. They were separated after two years. In 1883 he married Pretty Goods. They were separated also and he married one of Sitting Bear's wives, as at that time only one wife was permitted by government regulation. Sioux Woman was this wife's name and she died in 1890. Later, in 1896, he married Julia Bull Neck. Red Bear was made judge of the Arikara by Agent Jermark in 1915. He visited Washington in 1910 with Enemy Heart. Alfred Bear was their interpreter. He got his pension in 1911, through the efforts of Congressman Hanna.

ONE FEATHER

One Feather was born in the land of the Pawnee, on the southern trip described by Soldier, in 1832, and remained in that country until he was five years old. He recalls that on the journey to Fort Clark by way of the Rosebud and Yellowstone rivers a bear came through their camp. A baby in her cradle lay in his path and he bit her. The child survived but she was known when she grew up as Broken or Crippled Child. She was killed by the Dakotas at the crossing of the Knife River near the present County Seat of Stanton.

One Feather's father was Blue Bird, his mother, Young-White-Girl, and his grandmother, Young-Woman-Ahead. His father and mother both died of cholera at Fort Clark in the summer of 1851.

The Hidatsa and the Mandans sent eight horses and a peace pipe to ask the Arikara to come up to Fort Berthold, and they did so under the command of White Shield, Charging Bear, and White Horse. At the head of the Hidatsa delegation was Poor Wolf, and the Mandans were led by Crow's Heart (not the present one). They wintered at the Heart Camp and in the spring they crossed over the Missouri and built two villages.

One Feather became a warrior at Fort Clark and went on his first war expedition under the command of Soldier. About this time he suffered an attack of smallpox. He enlisted at Fort Stevenson in the second contingent of scouts. He was at the Custer fight and crossed the Little Big Horn at the lower ford and made his way through the timber and reached Reno's camp by climbing the steep intervening ridge.

One Feather was married first in Fort Clark village, giving for his wife a mule and a dressed elk skin. She died of measles on the journey from Fort Clark. Later he married, at Fort Berthold, his second wife, a woman of mixed blood (Arikara and Dakota).

RUNNING WOLF

Running Wolf was born at Fort Clark Village in the winter of 1856. His father was Gun-Pointing-to-Breast, and his mother was Chief-Woman-Village. His mother's father was The-Only-Crow-Head. Both his parents had smallpox at Fort Clark in 1837. He just remembers the Dakota attack upon the two Arikara villages opposite Fort Berthold. He also remembers a fight between the Dakotas and Arikara in the timber near the Fort Berthold village.

His first enlistment was in 1876, for a period of six months. This was all of his service in the United States Army. His first fight with the Dakotas was at the present site of Kasmer, Mercer county. He was then eighteen years old. The grass was just coming up in the springtime when three hundred Dakotas came to the bank and offered to fight, and the whole village, even some of the women, went across. It had been a long time since the Dakotas had come. Five Arikara, Bear-Turning, Bear-Going-in-Woods (wounded in U. S. service as scout), Little Crow, Standing Bear, and Black Shirt were killed. Foolish (Alfred Chase's father), a Mandan, was killed also, but no Dakotas were killed.

Running Wolf was married at sixteen to Young-Red-Calf-Woman. The first winter after they scattered from Fort Berthold, his mother died. Murphy was agent there at the time. His father had died much earlier at Fort Berthold. He was a member of the War Dance Society, now existing, before he was sixteen; at that time its head was Chief-White-Man.

GOES AHEAD, CROW SCOUT

Goes Ahead was born in 1852 on the Platte River, where the timber was very big. The Crows had smallpox and he was born in a party fleeing from this country on account of smallpox. His father's name was Many-Sisters. His mother was called Her-Door. His grandfather was White-Ear-Bear. At twelve he stole two horses during a raid to the Dakota country, near Forsyth. He was the first one to get back home. He fasted first at the age of twenty-two and celebrated his first sun-dance at the age of twenty-three, and carries the scars on his shoulders. His medicine was a coyote hide given him by his father-in-law. He once fought the Utes in the western country. He was never in Canada, but knew the country well south of the Black Hills.

He recalls that about 1873 a party of white men went through his country fighting with the Dakotas. They had pack-horses, picks, and shovels. They were fine shots and killed many of the Dakotas and took scalps. They wore war-bonnets and they gave some to the Crows, who were friendly. Among the men were four called Yellow Mule, Crooked Nose, Big Nose, Liver Eater. The two first named talked the Crow language very well and they were trappers and hunters in the Crow country.

JAMES COLEMAN

In the year 1872 Wilson and Dickey were post traders at Fort Lincoln. Major Dickey of this firm was the man for whom Dickey County was named. Their store was located at the ferry landing and James Coleman and George Harmon were clerks. The bookkeeper was a man named Perkins. Jack Morrow of Omaha was interested in the store.

James Coleman and John Smith went up the river on the Far West. This was the boat which met the army at Powder River, and it was commanded by Captain Marsh. On the boat were Captain Baker, and Company B of the Sixth United States Infantry. General Terry and one orderly were on board also. When the expedition reached the Rosebud, Terry restored Custer to his command.

John Smith was appointed post trader for the

expedition, for Custer knew and trusted him. He had been post trader at White Clay, South Dakota, and had made fifty thousand dollars there. Most of this sum was used to clear his brother at Yankton, who had killed a negro in a quarrel. John Smith bought about a hundred mules and did work hauling at the new post at Fort Lincoln. The store was at the mouth of the coulee and the mules were kept on the north side in dugouts. Most of the goods were taken on at Fort Buford, where Joe Leighton and W. B. Jordon were post traders. At the close of navigation the goods were freighted to Glendive and Miles City (Fort Keogh).

At Powder River Coleman was put off for a few days to sell liquor. Just a shelter tent was provided for the goods with partitions of canned goods separating the men from the officers. Canteens were filled only on an order from the captain. They held three pints and the liquor was sold at $1 a pint. No gold was used at all and the currency was in denominations of twenty-five cents and upwards. They received the liquor in forty-five gallon barrels and the finer brands were in bottles packed in casks. When the army moved the traders followed, going on boat to the mouth of the Rosebud where they again sold liquor. Then they went back to the mouth of the Tongue River, where Miles City is now, and Coleman has lived there ever since.

Smith made over a hundred thousand dollars before he left Miles City. At Bozeman he had a liquor palace, but the murder of a gambler at a card game in his place ruined him. He was later in Yellowstone Park selling liquor to the soldiers, and he died a pauper in a Sisters' Hospital at Billings, Montana, in 1904 or 1905. His son, Raymond, is in the Interior Department, Washington, D. C., and was called Buckshot. According to Coleman's report, the expedition netted forty thousand dollars from June to December, 1876.

After Custer's defeat, Coleman was on the boat with Terry at the mouth of the Little Big Horn, when Curly appeared on the east bank, a little above the mouth. He was lower than the boat. Curly held up his hand with a rag in it, and they waved him aboard. He wore a cloth about his head, a black shirt, a breech-clout, and moccasins. He came on board by the gang-plank. Coleman saw Curly make one sign, the sleep sign, once. Then a crowd of officers and men cut off his view. George Morgan, a squaw man (he had a Crow wife), who had a woodyard near the Muddy River, east of Buford on the Missouri River, translated Curly's signs and speech. He reported that Curly said he had crawled two miles wrapped in a Sioux blanket; that Custer's command was wiped out, and that Reno was in great danger. Terry sent word to Gibbon and Coleman saw a big dust following this relief column. After a while the soldiers arrived with mule litters of the wounded. One mule was hitched in front and one behind. Coleman stayed at the camp at the mouth of the Little Big Horn and sold supplies.

Steve Coleman, second cousin of James Coleman, was at Fort Randall in the United States army. He also carried mail from Yankton to the agency, and from Randall to Sully. He returned to Sioux City, Iowa, and recommended James Coleman for his position as watchman on board the government boat Miner, under Captain Hawley. This was in 1868, when he was about twenty years old; his duties were to watch on the boat after it was tied up, and call the mate and steward. The government was then building the fort at Fort Stevenson and at Berthold there was a village and trading post, also an agent named Courtenay. On one trip he remembers seeing soldiers at Fort Buford and a post trader named A. C. Leighton. Coleman went as far as Fort Benton, and returned to Sioux City on the June rise, the trip having taken six weeks. He saw both Reno and Benteen at Fort Rice in 1876.

INDEX

AMERICAN Fur Company, Fort Laramie station of, 20

Arikara, important part in campaign, 9-15; form U. S. Volunteer scouts, 11; Indian scouts with Custer's command, 26; discover Dakota village, 30; with Reno, 31; narrative of their part in the Custer campaign, 37; delegation goes to Washington, 38; story of first enlistment, 41; cede lands to United States, 42; attacked by Dakotas, 42; enlist as scouts, 45; in fight with Dakotas, 47; another enlistment, 48; further enlistments, 50; friends of Mandans, 63; earn money killing game, 73; read Dakota medicine, 78; interpret signs, 79 and *note*; anointed by medicine man, 84, *note*; list of those who rode to the charge, 85; led by Crows, 86-88; in battle of Little Big Horn, 93-121; carry messages of the defeat, 104, 105; drive off Dakota horses, 117; reported killed, 143; camp attacked by Dakotas, 148; charge for Dakota camp, 149, 150; fight with Dakotas, 166, 167, 168, 169; find gold, 169; visit the Pawnees, 179; winter at Painted Butte, 181; many die of smallpox, 181; warriors killed by Dakotas, 189, 190; go to Fort Berthold, 203

Armstrong, meeting of scouts, 9

Augur, General C. C., commands Department of the Gulf, 23, *note*

Arrow-Feathered-by-Crow-Feather, see *Coleman, James*

Bear, Alfred, interpreter, 121, 135, 163

Bear Chief, chief over Arikara, 37

Bear's Belly, scouts meet at his home, 9; story of expedition to Black Hills, 163-170; drags head and skin of bear, 199

Beauchamp, Peter, interpreter, 10, 37, *note*; goes to Washington, 38; present at meeting of scouts, 45; fights with Dakotas, 47; mentioned, 54

Beede, Judge A. McG., hears scout narratives, 9; mentioned, 12

Belle Fourche, Black Hills camp, 19

Benteen, Major, commands part of Custer's expedition, 31; ordered to join Custer, 32; meets Reno,

33; in battle of Little Big Horn, 94, *note*, 107, *note*, 122, *note*, 172, 173; mentioned, 209

Berthold, Fort, reservation, 9; mentioned, 44; attacked by Dakotas, 187, 188

Big Belly, Crow scout, 86; disputes with Custer, 92; in battle of Little Big Horn, 96, 97, 98, 99

Big Horn River, center for Indian operations, 24

Black Fox, enlists as scout, 51; battle of Little Big Horn, 119, 120, 122 and *note*, 150 and *note*, 155; disappears, 160; killed, 193

Black Hills, part of Dakota reservation, 17; gold discovered, 18; second expedition, 21, *note*; story of expedition, 163-170

Black Mouth, secret society, 186

Bloody Knife, takes prominent part, 12; sent on expedition, 49; enlists as scout, 51; Custer's favorite scout, 58 and *note*; promised many things by Custer, 62; orders to scouts, 74; stops quarrel between Reno and High Bear, 74, *note*; drunk, 78; his dress in battle, 96; body found, 109; scalp recognized, 111; in battle of Little Big Horn, 122, 123, 127, 129, 150, 151; shot at by Custer, 194

Bob-tailed Bull, first to fall, 11; mentioned, 53, 55; interview with Custer, 55-57; made leader, 56; meets Custer, 58; leader of Grass Dance Society, 59; leads band of scouts, 77, 82; in battle of Little Big Horn, 95, 96, 97,

98, 102 (killed), 122, 123, 126, 127, 150; made sergeant, 136

Bouyer, Mitch., interpreter, 158 and *note*; tells scouts to go with Custer, 159

Boy Chief, brother of Red Bear, 52; story of enlistment, 53-55; in battle of Little Big Horn, 95, 122, 130, 131, 150, 151, 154; continues narrative, 118-119; killed, 189

Bradley, Lieutenant, first of Terry's command to reach field of disaster, 107, *note*

Buffalo, secret society, 186

Bull Head, enlists as scout, 44; made head of band, 46; thrown from horse, 47; belongs to secret society, 48

Bull-Stands-in-the-Water, leader of Da-roch´-pa, 59; wants to go to happy hunting ground with a full belly, 83; in battle of Little Big Horn, 130, 131, 132

Burial scaffold, 75

Caroó, Dakota scout, 59; detailed, 69; in battle of Little Big Horn, 131

Chambers, Major Alex., commands troops, 25

Charging Bull, enlists as scout, 45, 50, 51; in battle of Little Big Horn, 130, 131

Clark, Fort, mentioned, 42

Coleman, James, white trader, 71 and *note*; biography of, 206-209

Commission, to treat with Indians, 17

Congress, provides commission to treat with Indians, 17; investi-

gation of abuses, 57, *note*
Crazy Horse, camp destroyed, 23
Crook, General George, commands Department of the Platte, 22, *note*; ordered to proceed against Indians, 23; driven back, 24; second expedition, 24; again retreats, 25; quoted, 81, *note*; unites with Terry and Gibbon, 146 and *note*; on Sitting Bull's trail, 147
Crooked Horn, enlists as scout, 51; meets Custer, 58; head of New Dog Society, 59; orders scouts to take note to camp, 88
Crow, secret society, 186
Crow Gizzard, Hidatsa chief, 42
Crow scouts, with the army, 76 and *note*; report abandoned Dakota camps, 80; in battle of Little Big Horn, 93-121, 123, 129, 130; reported killed, 120; return to reservation, 146, 147; meet Custer, 158; brought Terry first news of battle, 160 and *note*
Crows, lead the scouts, 86-88; in battle of Little Big Horn, 93-121
Curley, not sole survivor, 14, 15; with Custer at battle of Little Big Horn, 119, 120; not with Custer, 160; reaches mouth of Little Big Horn, 208
Custer, Mrs. Elizabeth, with her husband, 136, *note*
Custer, General Geo. A., his strategy, 13, 14; commands expedition to Black Hills, 18; at Fort Lincoln, 25; starts on last expedition, 26; receives instructions, 27; strangely depressed, 29; decides to attack, 30; first sees Indian village, 33; killed with entire command, 34; at Fort Lincoln, 48; finds gold in Black Hills, 49; called Long Hair, 51; interview with scouts, 55-57; summoned to Washington, 57, *note*; first on the march and picked out his own camps, 61; writes to Mrs. Custer of difficulties, 66, *note*, 67, *note*; reproves Howling Wolf, 73, *note*; marches to Tongue River, 75, *notes*; heart like an Indian, 77; asks opinions of scouts, 80; speech to scouts, 81-82; views camp of Dakotas, 91; disputes with Big Belly, 92; movements known by Dakotas (?), 91, *note*, 93; instructs scouts to capture Dakota horses, 93; fight was ended, 102; body found, 108; exhorts scouts, 121; calls for scouts, 139; visits scout camp, 140; his confidence, 149 and *note*; in the middle of the charge, 150; fought too soon, 157; meets Crow scouts, 158; planning next move, 159; expedition to Black Hills, story of, 163-170; permits a fight, 165; gold found, 169; consults with officers, 172; shoots at Reynolds and Bloody Knife, 194; punishes Isaiah, 195
Custer, Tom, brother of the General, 53; frightened, 90; visits scout camp, 140; mentioned, 172
Custer's Last Look, hill, 82, 108, 160

Dakotas, territory set apart for, 18 and *note*; hostiles, 22; attack

Arikara, 42; defeated, 43; scouts go along with Arikara, 59; make medicine, 78; inscriptions on sandstone, 79; abandon camps, 80; knew of Custer's movements (?), 91, *note*, 93; in battle of Little Big Horn, 93-121; women urge warriors, 101; dead bodies stripped by soldiers, 107, 109, 110; break up village, 117, *note*; attack camp of scouts, 148; fight with Black Hills expedition, 166, 167, 168; attack on Reno and Custer, 172, 173, 174, 175; retreat, 175; attack Fort Berthold, 187, 188; attack Fort Lincoln, 189

Da-roch´-pa, secret society, 59; Moccasin Game with Grass Dancers, 72

Death songs, scouts told to sing, 77

Doane, Lieutenant, constructs litters for wounded, 113, *note*

Dorman, Isaiah, negro interpreter, 75 and *note*; body found, 110; punished by Custer, 195

Duckett, Reuben, interpreter, 149

Elk Head (Not-Afraid-of-Anybody), enlists as scout, 44

Ellis, Fort, in Montana, 25

Expedition to Black Hills, story of, 163-170

Far West, steamboat, waits for wounded soldiers, 114, *note*; mentioned by Terry, 143, *note*; arrives at depot, 144 and *note*; mentioned, 206

Fetterman, Fort, mentioned, 23; troops march from, 25

Fight of horse and buffalo, 200

Foolish Bear, enlists as scout, 50, 51; in battle of Little Big Horn, 97; carries message, 134, 135

Foolish Dog, secret society, 186

Forked Horn, detailed on scouting expedition, 69; leads party, 82; in battle of Little Big Horn, 97, 98, 100, 101, 104, 105, 107, 110, 122, 123, 129, 150

Game, Indians earn money killing, 72, 192

Garreau, Pierre, interpreter, 42; mentioned, 188

Gerard, F. F., at Fort Stevenson, 44; aids Indian enlistments, 44, 45; at Fort Lincoln, 53; directs scouts, 59; tells Indians they can buy liquor, 72; tells scouts to sing their death songs, 77; gives scouts orders from Custer, 86; looks for Custer's body, 107, 108; directs scouts, 113, 114, 121; takes scouts to headquarters, 135; his story of the Custer fight, 171-175; mentioned, 182; sends Arikara to find gold, 183, 184; receives gold, 185; beats off Dakotas, 187, 188; mentioned, 191

Gibbon, Colonel John, commands division, 25; meets Terry and Custer, 26; with Terry saves Reno, 35; in camp, 72, *note*; quoted, 106, *note*; reaches battle field, 107, *note*; called Chief-with-a-Red-Nose, 145 and *note*; unites with Crook, 146 and *note*; mentioned, 208

Goes-Ahead, Crow scout, supplementary story by, 157-160; biography of, 205, 206

Gold, found by Soldier, 185

Goose, enlists as scout, 50, 53; favorite of Custer, 61; carries letter, 72, 73; in battle of Little Big Horn, 95, 96, 97, 98 (wounded), 99, 100, 101, 102, 104, 105, 107, 113, 114, 122, 123, 129, 150; detailed by Custer, 140, 141 and *note*.

Grass Dance, secret society, 59; Moccasin Game with Da-roch´- pa, 72

Gurley, Lieutenant, at Fort Lincoln, 48

HALF-YELLOW-FACE, chief of Crow scouts, 80, *note*; see *Big Belly*

Hidatsa, cede lands to United States, 42; send peace pipe to Arikara, 203

High Bear, enlists as scout, 51; dispute with Reno, 73, *note*

Hodgson, Lieutenant, headstone, 159

Horns-in-Front (Young Hawk's father), enlists as scout, 50; welcomes Young Hawk, 115

Howard, John, interpreter at Fort Lincoln, 63; goes with mail carrier, 64

Howling Bear, calls for recruits, 188

Howling Wolf, enlists as scout, 51; hides his horse, 73, *note*

Hudson's Bay Company, Fort Laramie originally station of, 20

INDIAN songs, death songs, told to sing, 77; war songs and marching songs, 136 and *note*

Indians, reservation for, 18, *note*; object to entering Black Hills, 19; hostiles and outlaws, 22; drive back Crook, 24; hundreds leave reservations, 24; stronghold on Little Big Horn, 26; concentrate on Custer's troops, 33; war chiefs in battle of Little Big Horn, 35; delegation goes to Washington, 38; cede lands to United States, 42; earn money killing game, 72; sundance, 78, and *note*; sign language, 79; fighting tactics described to Custer, 80-81; marching songs, 136 and *note*

Jordon, W. B., post trader, 207

Keogh, Fort, see *Miles City*

Laramie, Fort, old frontier post, 20

Left Handed, enlists as scout, 50; carries mail, 67

Leighton, A. C., post trader, 209

Leighton, Joe, post trader, 207

Lincoln, Fort Abraham, exploration party leaves for Black Hills, 18; near Bismarck, 25; cavalry stationed there, 48 and *note*; wounded arrive, 145, *note*; scouts arrive with letters, 149; Black Hills expedition arrives, 170; attacked by Dakotas, 189

Liquor selling to soldiers and Indians, 71, 72

Little Big Horn River, Indian stronghold, 26; battle of, described by Young Hawk, 93-121; news of defeat reaches Gibbon,

106, *note*; story of battle told by Little Sioux, 149-157

Little Brave, in battle of Little Big Horn, 96, 103, 122, 123, 124, 125, 126, 129

Little Sioux, enlists as scout, 50; in battle of Little Big Horn, 130, 131; supplementary story by, 149; biography of, 191-193

Long Hair, see *Custer, General Geo. A.*

Lucky Man, see *Reynolds, Charles*

McDougall, escorts pack-train, 31; joins Reno, 101, *note*

Mandans, delegation goes to Washington, 38; cede lands to United States, 42; friends of Arikara, 63; smallpox, 181; send peace pipe to Arikara, 203

March from Bismarck to the Little Missouri, story of, told by Running Wolf, 135-149

March from Fort Lincoln to Powder River, 57-63, 66-69, 71-85

Marsh, Captain Grant, in command of Far West, 143, *note*

Miles City, Montana, built on site of Dakota Camp, 75, *note*; mentioned, 207

Mutilation of bodies, only one, Isaiah, the negro interpreter, 110 and *note*

New Dog, secret society, 48

Not-Afraid-of-Anybody, see *Elk Head*

ONE FEATHER, enlists as scout, 50, 51; detailed on scouting expedition, 69; in battle of Little Big

Horn, 121, 122, 130, 131; born, 179; biography of, 203-204

One Horn, enlists as scout, 51; sent back with mail, 63, 137

One Stab, guide and hostage, 20

Only Brave, enlists as scout, 45

Ord, General E. C., commands Department of Texas, 23, *note*

Peaked Face, see *Varnum, Lieutenant*

Pope, General John, commands Department of the Missouri, 23, *note*

Porcupine Dens, where carriers exchanged mail, 54

Pretty Face, enlists as scout, 51; detailed with mule train, 85; in battle of Little Big Horn, 131

RED BEAR, sent on expedition to Mussel Shell, 49; enlists as scout, 50, 51; winters at Heart Camp, 51; story of enlistment, 52-53; carries mail to Custer's camp, 63-66; leads band of scouts, 77; in battle of Little Big Horn, 96, 123, 124, 125, 126, 127, 128, 129, 131; supplementary story, 121-135; biography of, 200-202

Red Cloud, his daughter wife of One Stab, 20; commands large numbers, 25

Red Cow, Mandan chief, 42

Red Dog, enlists as scout, 44

Red Elk, enlists as scout, 45

Red Foolish Bear, enlisted as scout, 53; sent back with mail, 63, 137; in battle of Little Big Horn, 96, 98, 102, 105, 107, 113, 122, 129

Red Star, story of march, 57-63, 66-69, 71-85; story of special scout work, 86-93; in battle of Little Big Horn, 94, 95, 122, 130, 131, 151; gives horse to Soldier, 117; continues narrative, 118-121; biography of, 195-200

Reno, Major, could have held position, 12; with Custer's expedition, 26; ordered to "charge the village," 31; saved by Terry, 35; dispute with High Bear, 73, *note*; "The man with the dark face," 74, *note*; in battle of Little Big Horn, 94, *note*, 95, *note*, 102, *note*, 103, *note*, 105, *note*, 115, *note*, 117, *note*, 119, *note*, 120, 122, *note*, 123, *note*, 124, *note*, 128 and *notes*, 129, 130, 150, *note*, 159; ordered to overtake Indians, 172; results of his tactics, 173, 174, 175; mentioned, 209

Reynolds, Charles, sent to Fort Laramie, 20; in Black Hills, 49, 50; called "Lucky Man," 86; sends note to camp, 88; at the cave or den, 164, *note*; sent with papers by Custer, 168; arrives at Fort Lincoln, 170; killed, 173; shot at by Custer, 194

Reynolds, Colonel J. J., with expedition to Indian country, 23

Rice, Fort, cavalry stationed there, 48, *note*

Royal, Colonel W. B., commands troops, 25

Running Wolf, enlists as scout, 51; supplementary story by, 135-149; biography of, 204-205

Scabby Wolf, enlists as scout, 51; carries mail, 67

Secret societies, New Dog, 48, 59; Grass Dance, 59; Da-roch´-pa, 59; Moccasin Game, 72; Crow, Foolish Dog, Black Month, Buffalo, 186

Sheridan, General P. H., in command of Missouri Military Division, 22 and *note*; orders Crook to proceed against Indians, 23; plans another campaign, 24; reports on Indian attacks, 48, *note*; quoted, 81, *note*, 92, *note*

Sibley's expedition, mentioned, 183

Sioux, see *Dakotas*

Sitting Bear, tells story of his father, Son-of-the-Star, 37; tells of first enlistment of Arikara, 41

Sitting Bull, leader of hostiles, 22; commands large forces, 24; not in battle, 35 and *note*; fights with Arikara scouts, 47; belongs to secret society, 48; makes medicine, 80 and *note*; offers to lead scouts, 188

Smallpox, kills many Indians, 181

Smith, E. W., assistant adjutant general, issues instructions to Custer, 27

Smith, John, post trader, 206; trusted by Custer, 207; died a pauper, 208

Smoke, see *White Ghost*

Soldier, enlists as scout, 44; continues narrative, 46-48; to look after rations, 46; fights with Dakotas, 47; interview with Custer, 55-67; second in command, 56; head of New Dog

Society, 59; leads band of scouts, 77; supplementary story, 115-118; wailing song, 115, *note*; in battle of Little Big Horn, 130, 154; biography of, 179-187

Son-of-the-Star, story told by Sitting Bear, 37; head of Arikara police, 37; called to Washington, 38; promises to furnish warriors, 40; asked for more scouts, 51; encourages scouts, 52

Stabbed, enlists as scout, 51; meets Custer, 58; carries letter, 72, 73; tells Custer Indian tactics, 80-81; exhorts young men, 84; instructs scouts, 93; in battle of Little Big Horn, 130, 131, 133, 154

Stevenson, Fort, built on Indian land, 43; meeting place for scouts, 44, 45

Strikes Enemy, in battle of Little Big Horn, 96, 97, 98, 99 (wounded), 101

Strikes-the-lodge, enlists as scout, 51; leader of Da-roch´-pa, 59; in battle of Little Big Horn, 130, 131, 154

Strikes Two, sent on expedition, 49; enlists as scout, 50; in battle of Little Big Horn, 94, 122, 130, 131, 132, 134, 150, 151, 154; continues narrative, 118-119; story of expedition to Black Hills, 163-170; biography of, 187-191

Sun-dance, Indian ceremony, 78 and *note*; mentioned, 205

TALL BEAR, enlists as scout, 44, 45; meets Custer, 58

Taylor, Joe, mentioned, 54, 193

Terry, General Alfred H., commands Department of Dakota, 22, *note*; at Fort Lincoln, 25; meets Custer and Gibbon, 26; saves Reno, 35; goes to mouth of Powder River, 68, *note*; quoted, 85, *note*; disbelieves story of Custer's defeat, 107, *note*; called Wearer-of-the-White-Hat, 134 and *note*; assumes command of the Seventh Cavalry, 135, *note*; in command of camp on the Yellowstone, 142, *note*; reports on Far West, 143, *note*; unites with Crook, 146 and *note*; called No-Hip-Bone, 157; hears of Custer's defeat, 160 and *note*; on Far West, 206; sends word to Gibbon, 208

Travois for wounded, 113; used for Soldier, 186

Two Bears, enlists as scout, 45

U. S. VOLUNTEER Indian scouts, posts found, 11

VARNUM, Lieutenant, chief scout, 30; discovers camp of Dakotas, 83, *note*; discovers pony herd, 84, *note*; in battle of Little Big Horn, 102, 107, 108; mentioned, 136, 146, 171, 197

Watkins, E. C., Indian inspector, 22

Wearer-of-the-White-Hat, see *Terry*

White Cloud, Dakota scout, in battle of Little Big Horn, 129, 130, 131; carries message, 134, 135

White Ghost (Smoke), enlists as scout, 44

White Shield, chief over Arikara, 37; represents his tribe, 42, 43; police force, 45

Woolly-Back, white commandant of post, 111

Wounded, carried on travois, 113, 114; placed on steamboat, 114; arrive at depot, 144; reach Fort Lincoln, 145, *note*

YOUNG HAWK, tells story of enlistment, 48; enlists as scout, 48; goes with Custer to Black Hills, 48, 49; tells of second enlistment, 50; again enlists, 51; leader of Grass Dance Society, 59; cooked for Custer, 61; detailed on scouting expedition, 69; story of the expedition, 69-71; narrative of, 93-115; expects to be killed, 95; seized with madness, 99; carries message of defeat, 105; angry at Custer's death, 108; in battle of Little Big Horn, 122, 123, 124, 129, 130; detailed by Custer, 140, 141; carries letters to Fort Lincoln, 149; biography of, 193-195